Child Prostitution in India

About the author

Joseph Gathia is Founder-Director of Centre of Concern for Child Labour and has been with media for a long time. As a Programme Officer with Indian Social Institute, Extension Services and Regional Coordinator of Terre des Hommes, Germany, India Programme, he initiated number of capacity building activities among NGOs. One such early effort by him was in Manipur in 1981. He is co-author of Women and Child Workers in Unorganised Sector (Concept, 1983) and Child Labour: An Analytical Study (1992). A postgraduate in literature and sociology, J. Gathia has major interest is changing paradigms of knowledge, the application of policy approaches in social empowerment through education and study implementation of foresights. He is keen follower of Nobel Laureate Professor Amratya Sen.

He has traveled to various interior parts of India as well as developed countries such as UK, USA, Germany, Japan, Italy, France, Canada, Australia, China, and The Netherlands. He actively participated in Vienna World Congress on Human Rights (1993); UN Social Summit, Copenhagen 1995, and World Congress on Women, Beijing, 1995. His major activities have been in the field of child labour, `invisibility 'of girl child in Indian sub-continent and social mobilisation for universalisation of elementary education. He has tried to bring vivid facts and problem of child poverty to the attention of the policy makers and political leadership. He believes that knowledge is power and education is the key to achieve that. He is closely connected with leading human rights organizations in India and has written extensively on the violation of children's rights in India and South Asia. He is recognized as one of the leading experts' on children's rights and his efforts between 1991 to 1995 set a new policy agenda with regards to child labour.

Child Prostitution in India

joseph gathia

Foreword by

Justice M N Venkatachaliah
Chairman, National Human Rights Commission
Former Chief Justice of India

CCfCL
Centre of Concern
for Child Labour

CONCEPT PUBLISHING COMPANY, NEW DELHI 110059

All characters are drawn from experience and field work. Names and details have been changed to protect identity.

ISBN 81-7022-771-2

First published in 1999

Child Prostitution in India
Gathia, Joseph (b:1946-)

Typeset & cover design
Akshay Wilson

Published and Printed by
Ashok Kumar Mittal
Concept Publishing Company
A/15/16, Commercial Block, Mohan Garden
New Delhi 110059 (India)

Phone: 5649024, 5648039
Fax: 091-(11)-5648053

For
those courageous
girls
who want to
break the
chains of servitude

"Mine are the tears
that froze with the pain
Mine is the pain
that has no name"

CONTENTS

Acknowledgements

I thank Dr. Ram Ahuja, former professsor of Sociology Department of University of Jaipur, Professor K. D. Gangrade, former Principal of Delhi School of Social Work, University of Delhi and Dr. K. K. Mukherjee, University of Delhi, Department of Social Work for the intellctual stimuli and critical remarks. Comments of Ms. Anuja Aggarwal, Lecturer in Sociology, Lady Irwin College helped me to clarify certain ideas expressed in this book. It is a great pleasure to acknowledge the help rendered by Dr. R M Pal, Editor, PUCL Bulletin, who contributed immeasurably by timely comments and encouraged me to complete my work.

Justice M N Venkatachaliah, former Chief Jusitce of India and Chairman, National Human Rights Commission has been a philosopher -guide to me. He critiqued my approach to children's rights with perception and intellectual sensitivity,and helped me understand the human rights philosophy.

AKM Anwaruzumma, Ms. Madhu Sharma, Uma, Pushpawati, Kamala, Bala, Ravi Magha and Visheshwar Singh Yadav helped me in the field work, and despite the hostile environment our field team carried out prolonged discussions with the community and later with the girls. I thank them. I thank Ratan Katyani and his colleagues of Rajasthan for all the help rendered to us during our field work.

Dia Mohan and Lalit Raizada rendered editorial help.I thank them.

And I thank all the people , especially an old woman whom I cannot name, for the many lessons they have taught me.

My wife and children attended to many details to make my work easy and they were my first critical audience. I owe them speical thanks.

For any lapses I alone am responsible.

joseph gathia

New Delhi
October,1998

राष्ट्रीय मानव अधिकार आयोग
National Human Rights Commission
सरदार पटेल भवन, संसद मार्ग, नई दिल्ली-110001 भारत
Sardar Patel Bhawan, Sansad Marg, New Delhi-110001 India

Justice M.N. Venkatachaliah
Chairperson
(Former Chief Justice of India)

FOREWORD

This work is yet another important contribution from Shri Joseph Gathia of the Centre of Concern for Child Labour. Children are our most treasured asset. Nearly forty percent of our demographic profile consists of children below the age of 14.It is a matter of regretful introspection as to how uncaring our society has been and continuous to be towards the underprivileged section of our children. Perhaps the most wicked and unpardonable exploitation of the child is its sexual abuse in the relentless pursuit of man's lust. Mere hard words break no bones. Society has to come face to face with this ugly and harsh reality and to take some hard decisions. This is a blot on our civilisation. With the continued merciless exploitation of the child, our pretensions to a civilised society wear thin.

Shri Joseph Gathia is an indefatigable, relentless and passionate fighter for the rights of the child. This report on child prostitution in India and case study of Alwar-Jaipur area of Rajasthan is candid. Shri Gathia himself recognises the enormity of the limitations on an endeavour of this kind. He speaks of the problems that a social worker faces, when pitched against the organised exploiters of flesh. Shri Gathia says, "Our choice of villages was restricted by their accessibility. We were unable to gain any information about child prostitution in any other community. While collecting the data for this study we also faced a great deal of resistance from some the middlemen. This was a direct result of a rumour that was spread that the families involved would be evicted if their reference came in the record. The flow of information about the movements of girls or women was severely restricted because no outsider was told about anything with regard to their closely guarded secret. The secrecy was all the more impenetrable because the clusters had single communities in them and accounted for homogeneity and unity. Besides, the internal situation is known only to a few m en and women."

Against these odds, Shri Gathia has done splendid job. He has grown two blades of grass where one grew and deserves the better of mankind.

New Delhi
October 27,1998 (Justice M. N. Venkatachaliah)

PREFACE

When I wrote Women and Child Workers in Unorganized Sector in the 1980s, I was attempting to understand the phenomenon of child labour.I asked myself why is this happening now? Thirty years of planning and Gharibi Hatao have not benefited the marginalised and the poor in our country. I found many clues in analysis of the culture. In 1986 during my trip to Nepal my friends informed me about the young girls being taken to India for prostitution. Most of the girls were from the seven Western districts of this Himalayan Hindu kingdom. Why from that particular area only, was my query to Nepali friends. Later on I discovered that age-old customs are being twisted by the pimps to push these tender age girls in the oldest profession of the world. On my return I realized that the problem exists in India too.

'Child Prostitution in India' study is my attempt to understand the direction of children's rights in one of the oldest civilizations and the one that gave the world 'Kamasutra'. The exact nature of the exploitation differs from one country to another. But the regional descriptions indicate there are some patterns in exploitation. Commercial sexual exploitation is a powerful industry built on abuse of power. Many children are from impoverished rural and remote areas where they and their families are least likely to understand the true nature of the risks and consequences involved and to be more easily deceived. But in South Asia like South East Asia a number of families usher their own daughters into this profession often in the name of custom or culture.

As I talked to the people, I became aware of how little information is really available about the world of the girl child in the families that profess prostitution. The girls were living in the world of their own.

As a rights activist I often felt bewildered and frustrated. These feelings led to questions: Why are these girls forced into this profession? Do they have any aspirations in their life? How can we help them? Why are drugs and alcohol so common among them? What do their mothers think?

In Beijing, concern for girls was reflected in the plan of action. During the last one-decade ECPAT and UNICEF have considerably contributed towards awareness raising at the regional and global level. The Stockholm Conference on Commercial Sexual Exploitation was the first serious international effort to move from statements of concern to actions. In India the National Human Rights Commission and the National Commission for Women both have included the issue in their list of priorities.

However, all these global and national efforts need a micro level understanding of the situation in different regions if they are to succeed. In many areas of our country girls are forced into prostitution in the name of religion or culture. What could we do to prevent it?

At first blush, it seems that things should be better now. After all, we have the women's movement. Hasn't that helped? The answer, as I think about it, is yes and no. Many things are happening but the girls today in India are much more oppressed. Their coming of age is dangerous for them. They face incredible pressures. As they navigate a more dangerous world, girls are less protected.

As I looked at the cultural practices that girls are forced to follow I was struck by what a girl poisoning culture it is in India which limits girls 'development, truncates their wholeness and leaves many of them traumatized'.

The book is an attempt to share my thinking with educators, health professionals, policy makers and any one else who works for and with girls. It is also for girls. The prostituted children (girls) know that something is wrong, but they tend to believe that there are no alternatives and that they are in safe place. Yes, they are birds in golden cage. I want to help them see their lives in the context of larger cultural forces.

I believe that many fellow citizens and many women personalities of our country are equally concerned about the issue. Sonia Gandhi,

Najma Heptulla, Margaret Alva, Chandni Joshi (UNIFEM), Dr. Mohini Giri (former, Chairperson NCW), Fatima Bibi (former member of NHRC and governor of Tamil Nadu), Jayalalitha, Medha Patkar, Kiren Bedi, Mamta Bannerjee, Amarjit Kaur, Vranda Karant, Rama Devi (Governor of Himachal Pradesh), Girija Vyas, Vasundhara Raje, Ella Bhatt, Mayawati, Vandana Shiva, Padma Seth, Pamela Philipose, Seema Mustapha to name few.

At the global level we have Hillary Clinton, who started US help for the third world girls, Catherine Lalumiere (Secretary General, Council of Europe), Mary Robinson (former President of the Republic of lerland and presently UN High Commissioner for Human Rights), Gro Harlem Brutdland (Chairperson World Health Organisation), Carol Bellamy (Executive Director, UNICEF), Sadako Ogata (former UN High Commissioner for Refugees) and Asma Jahangir (Chairperson, Human Rights Commissioner of Pakistan) among others, who are concerned about the situation.

Many others are also sounding alarms. What can we do?

We can strengthen girls so that they will be ready to face challenges. We can encourage self-protection. We can support and guide them. But most important, we can change the harmful practices of our culture with a view to creating a new society in which the girl child will be safe. Hope this book fosters a debate on how we can build that society

Centre of Concern
For Child Labour
New Delhi
October, 1998

joseph gathia

LIST OF ABBREVIATIONS USED

NHCR	-	National Human Rights Commission
NCW	-	National Commission on Women
UNICEF	-	United Nations International Children's Education Fund
ILO	-	International Labour Organisation
AIDS	-	Acquired Immune-Deficiency Syndrome
STD	-	Sexually Transmitted Diseases
HIV	-	Human Immuno Virus
ECPAT	-	End Child Prostitution in Asian Tourism
NGO	-	Non Governmental Organisation
CCFCL	-	Centre of Concern For Child Labour
ST	-	Scheduled Tribes of India
SC	-	Scheduled Castes of India
JRY	-	Jawahar Rojgar Yojna
IRDP	-	Integrated Rural Development Programme
DWRCA	-	District Women's Rural Community Action
NACO	-	National AIDS Control Organisation
WHO	-	World Health Organisation
DPEP	-	District Primary Education Programme
IPEC	-	International Programme for the Elimination of Child Labour
NAW	-	National Alliance of Women
CCFCL	-	Centre of Concern for Child Labour

LIST OF VERNACULAR WORDS

Dalal	-	middlemen
Was/bas/dhani	-	suffix for "our" settlement
Parivarik dhanda	-	family occupation (the euphemism for prostitution in these communities)
Gutka	-	chewable tobacco
Aanganvaris	-	child care centres
Sathin	-	village level woman worker
Lok junbish	-	peoples' education programme
Shiksha karmi	-	teachers' development programme
Balika	-	girl child
Ashramshala	-	residential school
Kachcha houses	-	mud houses
Pakka houses	-	brick and cement houses
Dhaba	-	roadside eating places
Bidi	-	handrolled leaf cigarette
Charpai	-	four legged rope woven beds

LIST OF TABLES

Chapter 1

Understanding Child Prostitution

" My entire family depends on me".

She said with a laugh as her alcoholic mother stood at the doorway ordering her back to the family's brothel.

A prostitute since she was 12, Chandrika expects to net the equivalent of $ 50 for the day's work. In an average month Chandrika figures she can bring home $ 500- an amount many of her customers don't earn in one year.

"My family, my brother, they sit around all day and do nothing," continued Chandrika, who has a five year old son from her initiation as a commercial sex worker.

"Everything they have is from me".

Far from the chaotic brothel of Bombay and Calcutta, where many children are kept in forced custody, Chandrika represents what many experts say are child prostitutes of India.

They can be found at truck shops, small town hotels and roadside tea stalls. They often do double duty as kitchen help and sex workers. And they have little choice when their parents, siblings and other relatives depend so much on their earning power.[1]

Chandrika was not duped or brought in the profession by coercive methods. She was not kidnapped from some far off remote area and brought to metropolis indulge herself in the oldest profession of the world. Instead her mother initiated her. Like Chandrika thousands of girls are confirmed in the name of tradition and religious practices - into sexual exploitation in rural India. They are victims of poverty, tyranny of caste and compulsions of harmful cultural practices.

"Some of these forms of child prostitution in India emerge from deeply rooted traditional practices and beliefs which still prevail," says Dr Richard Young, Chief of Community Development for UNICEF in India.

Definition

Before delving into the subject of `child prostitution' if would be necessary to understand the meaning of the two words `child ' and 'prostitution'- their historical and legal perspective and their connotations. First, let us discuss "child".

Child

In oriental societies 'child' has been described in detail in their varied literature. In the three ancient civilizations- Egyptian, Chinese and Indian- child has been the focal point of many paintings and has been depicted even on coins. However, it often meant male child thus relegating the girl child to the secondary place.

The expression child may be used in the following manner:[2]

- As a term denoting relationship as between the parents and their progeny.
- As a term indicating relative capacity to do something e.g. saying that a child cannot move a big boulder ,and
- As a term of special protection under welfare legislation like those prohibiting child labour and prostitution.

Interestingly there is no uniformity with regard to legal age of 'child'.[3]

Table 1: **Laws in India**

Indian Penal Code (1960)	Child usually refers to a person below 12 years
Juvenile Justice Act 1986	Juvenile for a male is some body who is below 16 years and for the female it is below 18 years
Child Marriage Restraint Act 1992	Child for a male is somebody who has not completed 21 years and for the female is below 18 years.
Factories Act 1958	Child refers to a person below 14years
Apprenticeship Act 1957	
Child Labour (Prohibition And regulation Act 1986	Child refers to a person who has not completed 14 years.

Source : J.Gathia ,Child Labour in India ,seminar paper for International Seminar on Child Labour, Monash University, Australia, December 1996.

Different laws interpret it differently. (see Table 1 above)

Such varying definitions under various laws notwithstanding the commonly understood norm describes `a person below the age of 16 as a child, between 16 and 18 as a minor and above 18 years a major. But the Immoral Traffic Prevention Act applies to all.(Amod Kanth, IPS, in Women and Children in Prostitution by Madhuri Joshi page 13)

In the common parlance child is a person, who because of his or her age, immature thought process and imperfect judgement, is unable to comprehend the consequences of his\her own actions. Such a person is called a 'minor' under the Indian law. One legislation is that a child may not be capable of forming any criminal intention up to a certain age and to that extent he\she enjoys immunity from any legal punishment. But beyond that age he\ she may be liable for his\her acts and face punishment.

A child of any age is not protected from torts. Present child images can roughly be divided into three categories, each stressing different actions to be taken:

* **Childhood can be considered as forming part of the private sphere and as a transition to adulthood. Here the stress will be on protection.**
* **Children can also be regarded as a separate group, a permanent stratum of society. In this approach, childhood is seen as a social and political phenomenon and the focus is on the balance of power between adults and children. Policy will be directed at promoting independence.**
* **The intergenerational perspective stresses the need to study and balance the needs and voices of different generations. Policy will therefore attach equal importance to protection and independence.**

One of the changes in our child image which seems to be taking place is an increase in attention to children's assertiveness and participation, leading to more stress on the views and feelings of children themselves.[4]

In general parlance the word 'prostitution' is used to describe the selling of sexual favours. Historically and generally, women are the objects of this activity, although there are male prostitutes and a growing number of prostituted children also. Oxford dictionary defines prostitutes as "person who offer himself\herself for sexual intercourse for money".

The word 'prostitute' has been derived from the Latin word prostibula or proseda. The houses of ancient Greek harlots were allowed to be opened in the afternoon. The girl stood or sat before the lupanaria to attract and entice passers-by. Therefore, they were called prostibula or proseda.[5]

The dictionary meaning of the word 'prostitution' is the act or practice of engaging in sexual intercourse for money and the word 'prostitute' connotes a person, usually a woman who engages in sexual intercourse for money.

The Suppression of Immoral Traffic in Women and Girls Act (1956) defines 'prostitute' as a female who offers her body for promiscuous sexual intercourse for hire, whether in money or in kind; and 'prostitution' means the act of female offering her body for promiscuous sexual intercourse for hire, whether in money or in kind.[6]

The Act was amended in 1978, wherein the definition of the word 'prostitute' was omitted and the expression 'prostitution' was redefined as the act of a female offering her body for promiscuous sexual intercourse for hire, whether in money or in kind, and whether offered immediately or otherwise and the expression 'prostitute' shall be construed accordingly.[7]

Mamoria defines prostitution as sexual union by a woman with a person who is not her husband, for some consideration in cash or kind and prostitute is a woman who sells her sexual favours indiscriminately and takes money or other valuables for each act of intercourse; and who has no psychic involvement.[8]

The gist of the problem is that "it is more or less a promiscuous sexual intercourse" that is; all women who are guilty of intercourse outside the marriage state may be regarded as prostitutes.

The important ingredients of prostitution, according to Weaver, are:

i) Promiscuity, barter and emotional indifference;

ii) It is different from the broader concept of sexual immorality due to the commercial nature of the relationship, and

iii) It is distinguished from illegitimacy, which invariably involves an illicit sex relationship but refers particularly to the production of a child outside the social approval.

There are many women, mostly from the first world, who claim it is their right to work as prostitute.[9] But the women from developing countries consider themselves victims of economic necessity.[10] Poverty can be considered the single most decisive factor that drives women into prostitution. But there are other contributory factors also. Prominent among them is the traditional practice of sexual slavery of women and girls.[11]According to A.C.Kinsey, a well know authority on sexual behavior" a prostitute is an individual who indiscriminately provides, sexual favours in return for money".

Child Prostitution

In the light of the above mention let us now understand the meaning of child prostitution. The United Nations Convention on the Rights of the Child, 1990, defines child prostitution as sexual exploitation of a child below the age of 18 for remuneration in cash or kind."[12] With respect to child prostitution and pornography the point of departure was taken from Vitit Muntarbhorn, then United Nations Special Reporter on the Sale of Children at the 48 th Session of the United Nations Human Rights Commission 1992.

'Child Prostitution' refers to the sexual exploitation of a child for remuneration in cash or in kind, usually but not always organized by an intermediary (parent, family members, procurer,etc.)

Pornography is public relations arm of sex industry. The child prostitution is closely connected with child pornography. It refers to the visual or audio depiction of a child for the sexual gratification of the use, and involves the production, distribution and or use of such material.

The factors that push children into sexual exploitation are numerous for example: economic disparities, inequitable socio - conomic structure, family disintegration, harmful traditional and religious practices globalization which undermines fulfillment of the basic rights of children.[13] By treating the child as a commodity which can be purchased, hired, sold or thrown away, the issue is no longer just a question of poverty, but rather one of values, in particular the values of consumerism. In 1970s, the Philippines chronic economic crisis led to make tourism a pillar of their economy. And because about 70 per cent of tourists were unaccompanied males, there was an unprecedented rise in prostitution and later of child prostitution.[14]

Some feminist theologians view prostitution not from a moralistic point of view but from a holistic perspective, taking into consideration the economic aspects of the problem. They see prostitution in women as the commodity of a country's prostituted economy. They denounce the patriarchal values that justify and perpetuate it. Feminist theologians go beyond welfare services. They lay emphasis on consciousness raising, theological reconstruction and economic restructuring that could lead to a fundamental situation to the problem of prostitution. For the purpose of this study child prostitution was distinguished from sexual abuse. It encompasses any pecuniary advantage (cash or kind) which is achieved by some party by the sexual activity . The sexual activity is not limited to the penetrative sex, or even to genital sexual activities

Types of Prostitution

There are different types of prostitutes : those who cater to local customers and these are usually poorly paid. There are young women who acquire " sugar daddy" who are generous in payments.[15] Prostitution has also been noticed popping up around military bases. Meerut, Agra, Siliguri, Bombay, Secunderabad., Machlipattanam etc. are examples in India.[16] Prostitution connected with tourism is the most institutionalized and the most lucrative. In the 1970s, Japanese package to the Philippines, Bangkok and Taiwan included hotel, golf facilities and sexual services of women all prepaid.[16] There is a special high-class prostitution catering to visiting businessmen. It is said to be part of the standard operating procedure of local subsidiaries to include these in their hosting obligation. They usually choose women from middle class families, especially students in elite colleges.[17]

Although cases of prostituted children is not new to South Asian region, child prostitution as commercial enterprise is relatively new.[18] The child prostitution may be found in a number of categories. It is therefore important to understand the phenomena and various types of prostitution which are prevailing in the society.[19]

First type are called 'Common Prostitutes'. These comprise the unfortunate women and girls who are recruited through pimps and procurers who have been sold or landed in brothels and vice-dens maintained by old prostitutes known as 'madams' and the pimps. Their induction into the trade is often through allurement, misguide about nature of work and many a time through false 'marriages'. If the pimps fail to win over the girls through other means then the procuring gang may resort to kidnapping and abduction. The recruitment methods and torture and the plight of this category of prostitutes is well documented by Sr. Rozario who conducted a study and interviewed 3,000 prostitutes in India. She says that (i) several young women and girls got into prostitution because they were raped and neither their family nor society was willing to accept them. (For example, a girl at the age of 12 was raped by her brother's friend who visited her and gave her the impression that he was in love with her .He gave her sweets and coloured ribbons. When she attained puberty at the age of 12, the boy said he wanted to marry her. He took her to a rented room, used her for a few days and then deserted the girl. (ii) Pimps are constantly on the look out for destitute willing to sell their children.

The Joint Women's Programme now has the proof of the fact that girls are sold by near relations on account of acute poverty. Nearly one third of the total population of prostitutes come from this source. A mother, in lieu of a sari, dedicated the child in her womb to Goddess Yellamma, should the child so born be a female and thus condemned her to a life of shame even before her birth!. A girl from Bihar who was sold just for Rs1,000 because she was raped and the family did not want to keep a girl in the house with a stigma.[20]

Dancing and Singing Women

This is a class in itself, who have a heritage from the Mughal period. They are drawn both from the Hindu and Muslim communities. Among them, the prostitution is handed down from mother to daughter as a profession with no stigma attached to a life of immorality. They are trained in the art of singing and dancing and the girls in the family are trained in this art from early age. As a matter of fact, a large number of them have acquired an excellence in the rendering of classical and semi classical music so much so that they have earned a place of pride and respect among the knowledgeable persons. They do not indulge in open prostitution and entertain or attend to very selected clients.[21] Their status is considered higher than that of common prostitutes. They also take pride in calling themselves as 'khandani'.

Patronised by Darbars

This class of prostitutes comprised beautiful women and girls who were raised by the kings and chieftains and landlords. They were well trained in the art of singing and dancing and were required to render special services for the rulers at the time of festivals to entertain audiences and guests. Sometimes, they had to enter into competitions with similar artist from outside and their excellence and performance had a bearing on the prestige of darbar. They were known as Kalvanathis', 'Mangalmukhis', and 'Nrityamangalis'. Seeing their face in the morning and at the commencement of a journey was considered auspicious. They had to become the paramours of princes or sardars or important courtiers of the state. Young men from the royal families used to visit them for learning the art of manners and behaviors and lessons on sex education. Their descendents are still found.

Call Girls

This phenomenon has grown with modernization and globalization. Dr. Promila Kapoor in her well acclaimed study on call girls in India gives fascinating and detailed account of this phenomena. Dr. Kapoor's book is a landmark study in India as far as call girls are concerned. Some hotel managements maintain their contact with society girls belonging to the elite or upper middle class families, who live in private houses very often quite educated.[22] They are well dressed, well mannered and enter into the trade not on account of any compulsion or financial constraints but for fun and extra income needed for meeting the expense of their luxurious life. They are called 'call girls' and are classed among voluntary prostitutes.

Mostly it is believed that girls above 18 would be involved in this trade but recent exposure in Japan indicated that large numbers of high school girls in Japan were engaged in selling their bodies for meeting their expenses. This trend needs to be watched in India as there have been cases when school girls were roped in sex trade through black mailing. The cases of Jalgoan (Maharshtra) Ajmer and Alwar (Rajasthan) are well known.

Religious Prostitutes

Religious prostitutes are known by different names e.g., Devadasis, Khudikar, Murloi, Basavi bhavin,Devali,Naikin and Jogins etc. They all start at an early age i.e. at puberty and prepuberty stage.[23] Brief description of categories of religious prostitutes is given below:

Devadasis : Though the term `devadasi' did not figure earlier than Chola times (850 AD to 1280) 15 it is largely believed that the practice started about the third century AD.. The term devadasi literally means servant (slave) Her duties comprise a combination of (a) propriety, (b) ritual (c) entertainment to assert positive fertility and prosperity. They on account of being married to god or goddess ,such as Yellamma or Mathamma were called 'Nitya Sumangali.'[24]

The system presently exists in Andhra Pradesh, Maharashtra and Karnataka and some parts of Goa. A girl whose mother is devadasi usually becomes a devadasi.

Jogins : The prevalence of jogins, a similar practice like devadasi continues in large part of Andhra Pradesh. In this system the girls are `married ' to God before puberty and they enter into prostitution when they reach puberty. In 1992 there were about 5,00 jogins in Nizamabad and 30,000 elsewhere in the State.[25]

Ganga a scheduled caste girl was initiated as a jogin around the year

1960 at the age of six. After eight years of initiation at the age of 14 a local landlord came and took her away at night and in a span of few years burdened her with a couple of children and paid a paltry sum of Rs 200 to her father by way of compensation and maintenance. After that she was passed on from one landlord to another till she died at the age of 30. The children left by Ganga are begging and the landlord has taken another jogin. There are about 10,000 jogins in the area.

Basavi : It means 'female bull' and it connotes the bulls freedom to wonder. Like Devadasis and Jogins, Basavis. Historically Basavis are forbidden to marry and expected to spend their lives performing religious duties. The system is known to exist in Andhra Pradesh and in scattered form in some areas of Karnataka. The Basavis do not immediately enter into life long career of prostitutes. They are still required to perform certain ritual duties. Since such work does not yield sufficient income they turn to prostitution.[26]

Dr.K.K. Mukherjee , an authority on prostitution studies in India refers to two more types of prostitutes : cage brothel prostitutes and Hitch Hiking prostitutes.[27]

Cage Brothel Prostitutes : They are mostly found in Mumbai and they are basically young girls. They are referred to as caged brothel prostitutes because of their virtual confinement to small cubical or cage like situation in brothels. All their earnings go to the brothel keeper till such time that the brothel keeper's investment is made in procuring them has been recovered.

Hitch Hiking prostitutes : They basically operate on road sides of national and state highways of Rajasthan, Maharashtra, Gujarat etc. They usually serve the truck drivers and fun seekers, moving in trucks and lorries. They operate on temporary and casual basis, often on contact basis, thereby bringing the element of call girl system, mostly under the guidance of an elderly prostitute or a brothel keeper.

The categories are not watertight compartment and inter mixture forms are also found. But one element is common ie., female sexual slavery in prostitution in one form or the other. Female sexual slavery is described as a condition which women and girls cannot change regardless of how they got into those conditions .

Cultural factors and prostitution

There are several groups in Scheduled Castes or Backward Classes who were traditionally professional entertainers. Today such groups have takeup prostitution as their main profession and they do not hesitate to profess that their source of 'livelihood' is prostitution. Although scattered throughout the country, majority of them are found in north and central India. They are Sanis, Bairas, Harias, Kanjars, & Sansis in the North India and Basavis, Harin, Baradas, Mang, Gurudus, and Dombars in the South India.

Impact of British Policies:

During early British Raj these caste groups used to supply food to the Pindaries in central and west India. They also carried messages and transported arms for them. But their main source of livelihood was singing and dancing. In fact, their role from 1830 to 1858 is not much studied. From the contemporary literature one gets glimpses of the services they provided to the participants of first war of Independence which British historians refer to as Mutiny of 1857. Many of these traditional groups which survived by dancing, singing and performing valuable rituals during the festivals faced hardship after1858. The land settlement system introduced by the British Raj virtually destroyed the peasantry in India and that was the beginning of the dark days of these cultural caste groups. Already 'outcaste' they were further haunted by the Raj through the Notified Tribes and Criminal Tribes lists. The policies of Raj made them pauper as they could not possess any land in any revenue village, they could not till the land and were to report to the police thanas, if they were to stay overnight in any village. This is still continuing. The police manual has not changed for them in free India.

Thus the process of liquidation through pauperization which was started in the British Raj ultimately left no options before these caste groups to adopt `prostitution' as mainstay of their livelihood. Hardly any research on these aspects has been done. Diaries of missionaries of central India do mention the plight of these groups but the Asiatic Society, which is prime source of anthropological material, is silent over these aspects. The system of prostitution as family occupation by these caste groups was cemented by the policies initiated by the British Raj. The present manifestation are only culmination of that process. More research in this area is required so that one gets deeper insight into the functioning of the cultural practices as push - pull factors of child prostitution in these communities. But the British policies cannot be solely held responsible for this. Many social reform efforts were undertaken by them - abolition of Sati was most prominent among them.

Role of Pimps

It is estimated by the organizations addressing the exploitation of women in prostitution that 80 to 95 per cent of all prostitution is pimp.Pimping is understood as 'living off the earning of a prostitute.'

A close analysis indicates that pimp control their women. Rape, kidnapping, physical abuse and torture are systematically practiced as form of control over women in prostitution by en Barry-!998)

An old prostitute in Alwar area stated that "Once a woman starts whoring for a man, there is no way out. The man wants more and more comfort out of such business at the cost of women."

Pimps control their 'women' in a number of ways. First verbal abuses and psychological terror that make women feel that they are worthless. This way the pimps keep the women or girls in a state of perpetual fear.

When the psychological weapons fail the pimps resort to physical torture. It usually starts with slapping and kicking in the abdomen thus rendering her unfit to carry her business alone. According to anthropologists Christina and Richard Milner, "A pimp wants his woman's mind more than her body."

Bollywood Glamour

Usually the pimps are well equipped with star - studded style of romantic images that popular television and movies have promoted. Pimps exploit girls' boredom that results from traditional female socialization, which leaves many young girls looking for some excitement and glamour in their lives.

Pimps look for and target young girls or women who appear to be naive, lonely and bitter and rebellious. Such girls and women are often runaways from their houses or from violent marriage. They are without jobs and normally in search of shelter. The pimp would play good Samaritan for days and weeks. For many girls it is a new experience: from neglect and scolding to caring and attention. Later on after making several obligations he will say "if you love me you will do anything for me." or "one time want hurt". This rational used by the pimp impresses the girl. She agrees and once she is in, it is endless tunnel into which she has to walk.

Some sociologists differentiate between 'man' and a pimp.(Elcaner Miller: Street Women ,1996). They distinguish between a 'man' and a pimp according to the number of prostitutes they have. A 'man' has one prostitute while a pimp has more than one. The 'man' will provide prostitution and will 'watch over' his 'woman' whereas the pimp considers himself more like a manager. Most of the prostitution is pimp controlled. The pimps are living off the sexual exploitation of women and girls using them as commodities. Some sociologists say that prostitution not controlled by the pimp is not sexual slavery. Pimp survives on the art of `procuring'. And from the torture stories that one comes across one gets the impression that procurement is most ruthless operation in flesh trade.

The practice used to, go far beyond the understanding of many. With market demanding younger and younger recruits, pimps look towards girls as a 'commodity' to be procured for the consumption. A report on child prostitution in India by UNICEF states that systematic trafficking from rural area accounts for a maximum number of girls in the trade.

Number - game

Perhaps most serious of these aspects is the way in which numerical data are presented and reproduced. Not only figures differ but also the different age grouping makes it complicated to compare the situation. One study estimated a total of 100,000,000 sexually abused children in the world, but did not distinguish between the categories of child prostitutes and sexually abused children.

Even in advance countries like USA the estimates present confusing picture. One study estimated that between 100,000 and 300,000 of young prostitutes are in USA (Snell 1995). Another study suggested that there are 2,400,000 child prostitutes (Joseph 1995). Similarly estimates of child prostitution in the Philippines varies: 30,000 (Moorhead, 1989) and 60,000 (Sachs, 1995). A map distributed by ECPAT gave in 1993 following estimated for various countries: the Philippines - 1.2 million street children and child prostitute 100,000; Vietnam- 40,000; Thailand- 200,000; Taiwan-100,000; China - total unknown estimated 5,000 in Sichuan Province; Sri Lanka- 30,000 prostitutes mainly boys; Nepal -150,000 girls in Indian brothels at least 20 % are under age; India - 1.5 million prostitutes with 20 % under 16 years (500-400,000 children) and Pakistan - at least 200,000 Bengali women prostitute, 20 per cent of them minor). But even the best estimates of the numbers of juvenile prostitutes may have poor statistical foundation. Nevertheless, because they are the only figures available, they are enter in the official records and are quoted.

In the early stages of our effort to understand this phenomena we approached officials and as well as some well known NGOs. The NGOs always said that it is 'increasing' and that the figures may be much higher. One group campaigning on the issue of tourism and child prostitution gives impression that due to foreign tourist the child prostitution in India is on increase. There is no reference to local clients. The officials were rather fair in their remarks and stated that no systematic data has been collected so far.

The National Commission for Women in 1997 initiated series of srtudies on child prostitution.This study brought out number of facts. One such study pointed out that the child prostitution is rampant in Andhra Pradesh and the girls who enter the profession at an early age accounted for 20 per cent of the estimated 5 00,000 families involved in prostitution as a profession. This finding of a survey commissioned by the National Commission of Women was reported in the Hindustan Times July 25, 1997. Referrring to the study on Delhi The Pioneer (21,July 1997) reported that "as many as 60 percent of the commercial sex workers in the Capital are children according to a study on child prostitution by the National Commission for Women". Dr.K.K. Mukherjee, Department of Social Work,University of Delhi, one of the key resource persons to the National Commission on Women in a study indicated that 62 percent of the women belong to Schedule Castes, 30 per cent to Schedule tribes and rest from other communities. (The Pioneer, May 10, 1997).

"Nearly 200 girls and women everyday enter this trade. Every year about 75,000 women enter this trade and 2/3rd is 66% not 80% two third of them that is 80 % come because of situational compulsions" (K.K.Mukehrjee, 1997). However, he further states that ' the number is an approximation because nobody has done an all India study'.

In India, out of 378 districts one third are drought prone areas and produce about two third of girls and women who come into prostitution and work in the metropolitan cities. (K.K. Mukherjee quoted in Trafficking of Women and girls for Sexual Exploitation, Joint Women's Programme 1997 seminar report published by William Carey Study and Research Centre 1997)

'The number is an approximation because nobody has done an all

India study. (K. K. Mukheree, Department of Social Work, University of Delhi,1997).

Despite quantum jump in information technology by India it is surprising that no systematic efforts have been made either by the Census authority or by the Ministry of Welfare to gauge the problem of child prostitution. I feel that the estimates currently hurled by the campaigners are either without reference to the sources or involve citing one of the texts that have gained credibility. The data on commercial sexual exploitation in India are lacking and the present estimates give only blurred categories. No doubt numbers play crucial role in shaping the public opinion because bigger numbers point towards the urgency and a overwhelming sense of priority but exaggerated figures can damage the cause altogather.

Even if the number is small the sexual exploitation of children is indisputable sign of a sick social structure, a society that can no longer perform even its most basic functions in the accustomed ways.[28] It is a society caught in the agony of most rapid and deep going economic and technological change. These changes are reaching deep into our personal lives, the enormous changes ahead will transform traditional family structures and sexual attitudes. They will smash conventional relationships between old and young. They will overthrow our values with respect to money and success. The future will unfold as an unending succession of bizarre incidents, sensational discoveries, implausible conflicts and wildly novel dilemmas. The problem of child prostitution cannot be viewed in isolation.

Notes and References

01.Stackhosue.J., In Rural India, Tradition of Child Sexual Exploitation Endure, Toronto Globe and Mail, Scrips Howard News Service, 1996.

02.Diwan.A., Children and Legal Protection, Deep and Deep Publications, New Delhi,1996

03.Kumar K, and Rani.P,. Offences Against Women Socio-Legal Perspective, Regency Publication, Delhi 1990

04.Verhellen.F,. Monitoring Children's Rights, Kluber Law International, 1996, page 7-19.

05.Varma P., Sex Offences in India and Abroad: A Sociological Study, B.R. Publishing Corporation, Delhi . pp 119

06. vide section 2(e) and (f) of Suppression of Immoral Traffic in Women and Girls Act (1956)

07.vide section (f) of Suppression of Immoral Traffic in Women and Girls Act No 76 of 1978

08.Mamoria C.B., Social Problem and Social Disorganisation in India, Kitab Mahal, Allahabad,1981

09.Notes at National Workshop on `Women and Children in Prostitution - Human Rights Perspective' organised by National Commission for Women and the Joint Women's Programme ,14-15 December,1995

10.Discussion with Promila Dandwate, a well known socialist leader of India and once member of Parliament. As a head of Samajwadi Mahila Sabha (socialist women group) she feels that one` cannot solve the problems of a sick society by giving medicine alone', what is required is prevention. She cautions that if we do not consider the effect of globalization and new economic order our efforts at preventive measures will not carry weight.She also forecasts that `in future women will voluntary prostitute than forced prostitute'.

11.Dr.Sarala Gopalan,(former Secretary, Department of Women and Child,Ministry of Human Resource Development. Government of India). Dr. Gopalan gave a thought provoking lecture at the workshop on topic` Rehabilitation and Consideration of Viable Alternative',1995 New Delhi. She played key role in Beijing confrence on women. Author witnessed her effots to include education for the girl child in the Plan of Action.During the Beijing conference the author on behalf of Centre of Concern for Child Labour organised a workshop on Girl Child Labour. The issue of child prostitution was discussed in that workshop. Dr Gopalan encouraged us to stress for educationand rehabilitation. Mr.D.S. Rai, District Collector, Raisen, Madhya Pradesh,one of the participants of the workshop in New Dlehi stated that in his district among a particular community any daughter can choose to be in the `profession' but once married she stops prostitution.But this happens to only 30 % of the girls.(proceeding of the National Workshop page 75, 1995).

12.U.N. Convention on the Rights of the Child, New York ,1990.

13.Ferze.Z, in Children and the Transition to the Market Economy Edited by Giovanni Andrea, and et la.UNICEF,1991 (page 69-89)

14.ECPAT Newsletters, 1992,Bangkok, Thailand
15.Background paper for the World Conference Against Commercial Sexual Exploitation of Child, Oslo ,1996
16.Mowli.V.Chandra., Jogin, Sterling Publishers, New Delhi, 1992
17. Kapoor, (Dr.)P. The Life and Work of Call Girls In India(1975), Vikas Publishing House, Sahibabad, India
18.Documents of UN World Conference on Human Rights, Vienna,1993.
19.Mukherjee K.K., Child Prostitution in India, Gram Niyojan Kendra, unpublished manuscript, 1997
20.Sr. Rozario.R., Trafficking in Women and Children in India: Sexual Exploitation and Sale, Uppal Publishers, New Delhi, 1988
21.Chopra S., human rights lawyer ,personal discussion in Allahabad,1996
22.Sr.Rozario.R., Trafficking in Women and Children in India, Sexual Exploitation and Sale, Uppal Publishing ,1988
23.Mukherjee.K.K., Child Prostitution in India,GNK, Gaziabad,1997
24.Karsenboom, Saskia C., Devadasi Tradition in South India, Motilala Bnarsi Das
25.Mowli V.C., Jogin, Sterling, New Delhi 1992
26.Lavanam.H., Sanskar 1992
27.Mukherjee K.K.,Child Prostitution in India, GNK,1997.
28.Ennew J., The Sexual Exploitation of Children, Cambridge, Polity Press,1986

Economics of Prostitution in India

Estimated number 900,000				**Transiction 37,000 crore**
Number	**Rs.**	**One day**	**Days in a year**	**Total**
400,000	50	20,000,000	200	4,000,000,000
300,000	100	30,000,000	200	6,000,000,000
100,000	200	20,000,000	200	4,000,000,000
50,000	500	25,000,000	200	5,000,000,000
40,000	1,000	40,000,000	200	8,000,000,000
10,000	5,000	50,000,000	200	10,000,000,000
900,000		**185,000,000**		**37,000,000,000**

* Estimated minor prostitutes (30% of total)
270,000 11,100,000,000

Total earnings (rupees) 1110 crore

The above estimates are based on the information collected from various sources: Patita Udhar Samiti (President - K. L. Bhola), JWP, ICCW, Nirmala Niketan, various journalists and some persons connected with the underworld.

Chapter 2

Review of Literature

The study began with a review of available literature on child prostitution. Soon we realized that the topic is blended with sexual abuse of children. And that few studies spoke in detail of child prostitution. Much of the material we came across was linked with the sex tourism and mainly related to the Philippines and Thailand. The material that we studied indicated that the issue of child prostitution is treated differently in different geographical regions of the world. Very little information is available on the situation in Soviet Union and Eastern Europe, though newspaper reports point towards rampant commercial sexual exploitation of children. Likewise, hardly any publications on child prostitution in China are available in India. In Latin America, the studies and campaign material are dominated by `street children' and the model of Latin-American street child is predominant in all developing countries including India. Literature received from Africa mostly from EDNA and APPCAN indicates that the focus there is on AIDs, child soldiers and genital mutilation among girls. So very few studies have been undertaken on child prostitution.

The South-East Asian literature is mainly a discussion on the concept of `childhood'. In case of the Philippines as well as Thailand the approach is of condemning foreigners for the evil of child prostitution. The cases cited in most publications are of urban areas mostly related to Bangkok, Pattaya and Metro Manila. The publications of End Child Prostitution in Asian Tourism (ECPAT) seems to have influenced most of the publications on child prostitution in India. `The Child and the

Tourist' (O'Grady 1992), and `The Rape of Innocent' (O'Grady,1994), are two books that have greatly influenced the literature of NGOs in South and South-East Asia. Many of the publications are of campaign and awareness raising type. Among the books, pamphlets and papers brought out by non-governmental organizations, no doubt the ECPAT contributions are outstanding in highlighting the plight of prostituted children.

A search in the libraries indicates that the literature from the Anglophone West (USA, Canada Australia and Western Europe) is more research-oriented. There is a marked difference in the tone and content of research material and the media coverage. The media stuff was sensational and was jargon- oriented in the late seventies. From 1980s the stuff is serious and has helped shape public opinion to the extent that many governments of the developed countries included this issue in their development aid programmes and foreign policy. British Foreign Secretary Mr.Robin Cook announced special programme to end child abuse including child prostitution in May1998 and signed first ever Memo of Understanding with the Philippines.

In South Asian literature the theme of `girl child' predominates the scene. The stress is on the more vulnerable aspects of female sexuality and thus emphasis is not only on the oppressive aspects of tradition but also pivots on the notion of the women and girls as objects as in trafficking. Books like Bahini (Joint Women Programme,1989), Trafficking in Women and Children in India (Sr. Rita Rozario,1988), Report on the National Seminar on the Girl child (Janssens-Sannon.P., 1989); Child Prostitution in Nepal (Rupa Dhital,1992); Prostitution of Children in Pakistan (Asma Jahangir 1986) ; Child Labour and Child Prostitution in Sri Lanka and the Legal Control (Goonasekere.S. and Abeyratne.A 1986), Boy Prostitution in Sri Lanka (Bond T.1981) gives reader the exposures in the problem of commercial sexual exploitation of children in the South Asian.

Some newsletters which are brought out by the NGOs mainly for campaign purposes and awareness raising were also examined. The ECPAT Newsletters (1992-93), Equations publications (1995-1997,

Bangalore, India) and material from Joint Women's Programme were examined to understand the thrust and arguments with regard to child prostitution. Surprisingly Gram Niyojan Kendra has produced very little material for mass awareness. As they are leading research group on prostitution they are in a better position to do so.

The material on campaign against child prostitution draws the picture of small children being sought out and exploited by Western tourists. The NGO literature available in India though not necessarily produced by the Indian NGOs virtually does not refer to the academic literature. The common theme which runs in the NGO literature is that the small girls are being sought by the foreigner for sexual exploitation. (see a newspaper coverage included in this chapter elsewhere) The age distinction is not clear and they often use word `minor' which may mean girls less than 18 years but not necessarily below 16. The literature also lacks distinction between various age group and barring few majority tend to make sweeping remakrs. There may be small number of foreign male tourists seeking sexual pleasure with tender age girls\boys but the exploitation cannot sustain itself without local clientele. The NGO literature is `silent' on the local clients.

In Bangladesh, Nepal, India, Pakistan and Sri Lanka the literature produced by the non governmental organisations hovers around three themes: the girl child, religious prostitution and trafficking for sexual purposes. In India and in Nepal the 'girl child' discourse focuses on religious prostitution (of which Devadasi is the best known form) and trafficking in children, while in Bangladesh, the rape of pre-puberty girls hired as domestic servants is an important theme (Blanchet, 1996, p. 119). In Baluchistan and the North West Frontier provinces of Pakistan, much of the literature on the girl child mainly highlights how the law looks at the problem. (Jahangir A., 1986).

Religious prostitution is practised in various parts of India and Nepal. Devadasi like cults are found in Southern India and also practised in other parts of the country. They derive customary sanction. Pre-puberty girls aged between five and nine years, from poor, low-caste homes, are dedicated by an initiation rite to the deity in the local temple during full moon. After a girl is married to the deity by the tali rite, she is branded with a hot iron on both shoulders and her breast. She is then employed by the temple priest. Sometimes, even before menarche, she is auctioned for her virginity, the deflowering ceremony known as `udilumbuvadu' becomes the privilege of the highest bidder. The market value of a girl falls after she attains puberty, when she is said to have no recourse other than prostitution. Yellama is represented as the principal goddess who is worshipped but, as recent research has shown that other deities such as Meenakshi, Jagannath and Hanuman are also propitiated. Religious prostitution is known by different names such as Venkatasani, Jogini, Nailis, Muralis and Theradiyan (Bahni, 1989; Marglin, 1985; Mowli, 1992; Story, 1987).

In Nepal, particularly the western parts, religious prostitution known as Badini and Jhuma is also practised. Although little is known about these practices, they do not seem to vary significantly from Devadasi. However, the main sexual exploitation issue in Nepal is the trafficking of girls to India. The open border between the two countries makes it difficult to monitor the movements (Human Rights Watch, 1995; O'Dea, 1993; Rozario, 1988). It is also stated that, because of corruption, official assistance is given to the sale and the trafficking of young girls (Agroforestry Report, Kathmandu, 1990). In most accounts Bombay is given as the main destination. The international trade routes most frequently mentioned are from Nepal and Bangladesh to India, and from India and Pakistan to the Gulf countries.

Different Phases

In colonial India some efforts were made to highlight the plight of women and young girls but they were part of study of traditions like Devadsi. After 1950s some studies were made but mostly contented with the Devadasi system (Shorth.J., The Bayadere or the Dancing Girls of South India: Notes for the Anthropological Society of India,1867- 68,Unpublished, India Office Library. In 1909 Edgar Thruston and K. Rangachari wrote `Castes and Tribes in South India' which is based on ethnographic notes of the Devadasi cult. The book describes `Devadasi' as low caste married women practising `sacred prostitution' and there is a detailed discussion on the laws of maintenance, presumably to help colonial administration. Not much is said about their life style. The colonial administration patronised the institution of `nautch girls'. The book provides very sketchy details. We found that in the first two decades of the twentieth century for there is virtually blackout of of research on sexual exploitation of women and young girls in India. In 1922 James Frazer came out with "The Golden Bough: A Study in Magic and Religion" (London,1922) giving brief passing reference to 'sacred prostitution'. However, a classic work by N M Panzer, The Ocean Story (translated by C H Tawney in ten volumes appeared in 1924. It is a classic work and is an account of a love affair between a courtesan-prostitute and a married man. It is a translation of Sanskrit Play Katasaritasagar. Appendix XI of Volume I, contains details on 'Sacred Prostitution'. It gives the reader an insight into the position of women in the third century BC. It is a valuable literary source.

The second phase of literature on the subject could be fixed from 1930 to 1950s. During this period much of the literature is influenced by the freedom struggle and writings of Balgangadhar Tilak, Gokhle, M.K. Gandhi, Jawaharlal Nehru, M.N.Roy, C.Rajagopalachari, M.M Malaviya, and Ranade to mention a few. It does refer to the plight of women in general. In the research field the focus was more on tribals. `The Aboriginal- So called-and their Future', Ghurye. S (1943) Gokhle Institute of Politics and Economics; The Warlis, Save.KJ (1945)Bombay; The Savaras of Orissa S N Roy (1927) Man in India; are some of the literature which reflects the concern of the time.

In the literature of third phase from 1957 to 1979 (International Year of the Child) we noted little more emphasis on the girls problems Note on Dancing Girls (Nachni) of Purulia, Gopa Bannerjee (1973),Man in India; Community of Dancers in Calcutta, Manjusri Chaki Sarkar,1972,Calcutta; The Gond and Bhumia of Eastern Mandla, Stephen Fuchs (1960) Asia Publishing House; Girl Student in Jaipur, Gora Vreede De Steurs; The Power of Tamil Women by Susan Wedly are some of the memorable readings of that period.

From Internationai Year of the Child in 1979 to;1989, year before UN Convention on the Rights: of the Child was adopted, a sudden spurt is notice of advocacy and awareness raising type of literature.But this was also the period when much of the activities in the field of CEDOW took place. So much of the literature refers to the violence on women with sprinkling references to girls. Nevertheless, much of the literature on exploitation of girls was written during this period. Bhattacharya, Mitra (1988) A Probe into the Personality of Adolescent Bengali Girls of Calcutta; Devasia Leelamma (1981), Female Criminals and Female Victims: An Indian Perspective, Nagpur,Dattsdons; Women in India: National Perspective Plan for Women, Ministry of Human Resource, Govt. of India. New Delhi; Khan, M Z and Krishna K.P.,(1985), `Cultural Familial Antecedents of Violence Against Women in India", India Journal of Psychology; Pereti P.O., and Cozzens, N.,(1983), Characteristics of Female Raped Not Reporting and Reporting', Indian Journal of Criminology; Raghvan CG and P L Bhandari(1989) Offences Against Women, Trends and Sheikhta Shehnaaz(1988)The Muslim Women's Rights Project", Lawyers Collective; Shukla and Saxena ,(1987) Women and Crime - A Perspective, Sage Publications; Seminar Special Issue (1988) Sati; Srivastava,S.P.(1978) Rehabilitation of Fallen Women; Srivastava,TN.,(1985) Women and the Law .New Delhi Publishing House; and Varghese. Jamila, (1980) Her Gold and Her Body, New Delhi Vikas Publishing House are some outstanding work of this phase.However,this is not exhaustive list .Other literature focusing on the girl child are Trafficking in Women and Children, Sr.Rita Rozario(1988,Uppal House, New Delhi); Women and Child Workers in Unorganized Sector,Gangrade KD and Gathia.J.,(1983,Concept Publishers,New Delhi) and Bahini (1989, JWP,New Delhi).Sr.Rozario's book remains one of the base reference on the child prostitution in India and Nepal.

After 1990 with the coming of the CRC into existence the content and the tone of literature in India also changed. The emphasis from 1989 till 1998 is on exposure and programme implementation and identifying loopholes in the laws. An important essay was written by Sheela Barse `The Girl Child' (1990) in which she highlighted prejudicial practices affecting girls, such as feticide, infanticides, neglect, nutrition lack and denial of education. January 1991 issue of The India Journal Social Work (Vol. LII Number 1) contains valuable reference material and deals with the status of the girl child. Priti Patkar's article `Girl Child in the Red Light Areas' throws light on the situation of daughters of prostitutes. This article raises number of issues having policy implications. `Jogin' (Mowli ,1992) ;Devadasi Cult (Shankar.J.,1994); Offences Against Women, (Kumar & Rani,1996); The Female Child in Family Setting (Anandalakshmi .S.,1991); The History of Marriage an Prostitution: Vedas to Vatsayan, (Sinha SN., and Basu NK,1992); and Family Rights of Girls, (Kaushik,S.,1993) are some of the important research which gives us an insight of the problem.

We feel that Vibhuti Patel's article `Depths of Degradation' (The Hindu,1990) will remain on the shelf of any researcher on this topic for a very long time. But then the contribution of Indian print media is an interesting area to trode. The Indian Press has contributed a lot in making policy framers to take note of this problem.

From 1995 much of the literature available on child prostitution with Indian NGOs and advocacy groups are either from the Philippines (mostly church groups) or from Thailand ECPAT office. Some material is very good from social awareness and advocacy point of view. They also convey the global linkages. The two UN agencies the UNICEF and the ILO are also circulating literature on child prostitution. Recent publication by ILO, `Intolerable Form of Child Labour' is an excellent material on the subject.

The Power of the Press

More than three decades ago Bernard Cohen Wrote:" The Press may not be successful in telling people what to think, but it is stunning successful in telling its reader what to think about.". The media do not change the importance of humanitarian crisis, but they significantly affect their impact (Edward Behr, Anyone Here Been Raped and Speaks English? A Foreign Correspondent's Life Behind the Lines (London,1992).

Press View of the Prostituted Children

Indian print media has been in forefront in raising the issue of human rights, be it a case of blinding of a Dalit girl in Tamil Nadu or denial of admission in the schools to the children of women in prostitution. The issue of child prostitution caught attention of media after a case against a pedophile was registered in Goa. However, some daily newspapers in India such as The Telegraph (Calcutta ,1992) The Illustrated Weekly of India (Times of India Group,1992), India Today (1989) The Indian Express (Sept. 1991) and The Hindustan Times (1989) were quick to comment in their paper on this crime against humanity. The Week (a Malyalam Manorama group of publication did a lengthy cover story on Child Prostitution in August,1996. This is a good example of treatment of the sensitive subejct. Similarly The Pioneer from 1996 till date has been giving prominence to this issue.

The Statesman (Calcutta) has been quite forthright in its attack on the system and for neglecting the development of children. The media coverage of child prostitution issue received boost when the World Conference Against Commercial Sexual Exploitation of Children was organised in Oslo 1996. So far so good. However, sometimes we come across some items in the newspapers which raises questions whether such coverage would do good to the cause in the long run. Below are some examples. (see box 1 to 5)

Box 1

` Many Dalits taking to prostitution'

New Delhi: Most of the women who enter into prostitution are Dalits. Dr.Mukherjee of Gram Niyojan Kendra said on the concluding day of the two day seminar on Prostitution and Prevention Action.
A recent study revealed that 62 per cent of the women belong to Scheduled Castes,30 per cent to Scheduled Tribes and rest to other communities.

(The Pioneer 10 May ,1991)

Box 2

Pune Children at tourists' mercy

Child prostitution thrives in city

Pune,April 27:Foreigners and outstation businessmen are the biggest clients of child prostitutes in the city. With an increase in the number of HIV-infected adult prostitutes in the city, children are now much in demand with those who visit Pune.

According to information available, children as young as six year old are picked up by the tourists. They are not too interested in children above 14.

"An increasing number of children, both boys and girls are being kidnapped to be supplied to the foreigners and businessmen. The parents lodge a complaint that their child is lost. But how many of them are actually found" asked the source.

(The Asian Age, 28,April ,1997)

Box 3

60 % sex workers are children : Study

New Delhi: As many as 60 per cent of the commercial sex workers in the Capital are children, according to a study on child prostitution by the National Commission for Women (NCW).

The study titled The Lost Childhood and based on a survey of 28 brothels on G.B. Road , identified as a red light area, says that there is a great demand for children in the commercial sex trade in cities like New Delhi where the population is growing day by day.

" There has been an upward trend in the supply of children, especially from the Advasi and Dalit sections ,the study adds.

The Pioneer, 21 July 1997

Box 4

Mumbai now has 70,000 vulnerable children walking on streets

Child prostitution on rise with AIDs

Mumbai:Dec 6: The fear of AIDs and superstition has greatly increased the number of children and young virgins being forced into prostitution in the red light areas of Mumbai.
A detailed study conducted on child prostitution by the Central Advisory Committee and the Indian Health Organisation has revealed the shocking statistics that one is five prostitutes in the metropolis are children under the age of 12.
A further 20 percent are aged between 12 and 18 half of whom become prostitutes when they were minors.
For shocked lawmen and legislators to make the difference, the problem is not hidden, more than 70,000 child prostitutes ply their trade on the stress of Kamthipura and Faras Road

Their number are growing at analarming rate of 30 per cent every year.

The Asian Age,Dec. 7,1996

Box 5

Mumbai Age Special

IHO stratstics regarding child prostitutes are as follows

City	*Population*	*Child Prostitutes*
Mumbai	12.4 million	70,000
Calcutta	11.0 milllion	50,000
Delhi	10.0 million	20,000
Pune	3.0 million	20,000
Nagpur	1.5 million	10,000

The Asian Age,Dec.7,1996

A close scrutiny of the news reports indicates that (i) the media prefers statistics to any general observation to convey the dimension of the problem, and (ii) the headlines convey the message in a very straightforward manner. However, a dispassionate analysis indicates flaw not in the coverage by the media but in the content provided by the concerned survey agency.

For instance, in the news item in box1 percentage of women froma particular section of the society are going in for prostitution. However, the study does not take into acount the growing phenomenon of call girls which is increasingly attracting women a nd youn girls from comparatively higher strata of the society.

Thus the impression conveyed is that the women and girl prostitutes belonging to that particular segment of the society are entering the pofession of their free will and choice and without any inhibitions.No monitoring factors have been identified.Mention of such information would have helped make an exhaustive assessment of the magnitude of the problem.

The story in Box 2 is terribly frightening for it opens with the sentence that conveys that all foreigners and businessmen who land inPune, straightaway make abeeline in search of child prostitues. If an ordinary housewife whose husband has gone ot Pune gets panicky on reading the news item, it would be understandable.

Also, the entire story is based on `according ot available information'. It does not indicate whether the source is official or private though the contents are spicy and horrifying. The story may be true but it needs to be backed up by facts to lend credence.

Anybody would be shocked to read the story in Box 3 that as many as 60% of the commercial sex workers in the national capital are children.

The study is based on a sample survey of only 28 brothels located in the red light area of Delhi and does not take into account the totality of the picture. The figures may be true as far as the brothel houses are concerned but to generalise it on the whole city does not help the cuase.The capital city with a population of an estimated 10,000,000 poplulation and would therefore require sampling from other parts of the city also. Further, the story also talks of an upward trend in the supply of children especialy from Dalits and Adivasi section but no comparative figures have been given to explain the phenomena.

One gets jittery after reading the news items in Box 4 and Box 5. While the reporter has done a good job in highlighting the concern, the providing organisation- Indian Health Organisation- seems to be hurling figures without any comparison. For instnce, it says that the number of child prostitutes is growing at an alarming rate of 30 % every year. What is there basis of such a claim or what is the benchmark year in whose comparison this increase has been noticed.

In most cases the facts supplied by the research agencies or the NGOs through the survey seem to be a case of `raw' data. The comparative figures ;and the time span are necessary in the reports. As such, in the absence of these ,it becomes difficult to understand within how much period the number of child prostituees has increased.

The objective appears to be to heighten public and policy interest in the issue by stressing the scale of the problem. But the important point is not the scale of the problem but its degree of seriousness as a violation of the fundamental rights of human person. There is also tendency to provide raw number such as '78,000 child prostitutes in Mumbai', does not actually provide an idea of scale. To do this one would require some knowledge of source, time, relative location and proportion. In many studies age is not clear or defined. The data on child prostitution not only widely differ but also vary depending on the thrust of a particular group or non-governmental organisation.

There is also reproduction and repetition of myths without proper explanation. Some claim the number of child prostitutes is growing at an 'alarming' rate. Yet no reason is given for this except for the fact that customers are turning to younger prostitutes because they believe them to be AIDs free. Before the AIDs all over the world it was repeated that child prostitutes were sought after because they were believed to be free of sexually transmitted diseases (STDs) . But much before the fear of AIDs spread there was widespread saying that penetrative sex with chidren would cure them of sexually transmitted diseaes. So one needs to ask questions what are the other reasons that suck children in world's oldest profession.

The literature reviewed here cannot be said to be comprehensive. However, it does highlight the main studies carried out so far. The dismal low level status of women in Indian subcontinent is frightening. Further, many texts concentrate on child prostitution with HIV\AIDS but there is very little matter on other sexually transmitted diseases. Some literature points towards loopholes in legal approach and incapability of law to punish the perpetrators of child sex exploitation.

Majority of the groups in South Asia see the problem of child prostitution as a phenomenon in its own right. But after the World Conference on Commercial Sexual Exploitation of Children in 1996(Oslo) the scene is changing. In my view this is a great contribution of the Oslo conference.

Many texts lay stress on degrading aspects of child prostitution, including being forced into it, raped by pimps, terrorized by gang members and becoming dependent on drugs (Sawyer, 1988; Tate, 1991). There is reference to the apparently inevitable links between prostitution and the use of heroin. Yet there is little information on long-term effects because there is no systematic research on the consequences of prostitution practised in childhood. It is simply concluded that juvenile prostitutes end up either dead or living worthless lives (Poffenberger, 1988). However, longitudinal studies do not seem to have been carried out.

Large numbers are considered crucial by many NGOs in their campaign because they convey a sense of urgency and an overwhelming sense of importance. Campaigns and journals tend to use them, without realizing the implications. Once used by the media these gain credibility. A study claims that there are one million sexually exploited children in Asia. Some interpret this as one million prostitutes. Many NGOs quote higher figures to catch the eye. Several NGOs say it is 'increasing', usually at an 'alarming' rate. Yet no reason is given for this except for the 'fact' that customers are turning to younger prostitutes because they believe them to be AIDS free. (Jubilee Action Trust, Lee-Wright, 1990; Muntabhorn, 1992; O'Grady, 1992; 1994).

Due to vigorous campaigning by the ECPAT, the issue of sex tourism and its linkages with child prostitution has captured media attention. (Asia Partnership for Human Development, 1992; Anglican Synod of Australia, 1993; O'Grady, 1992; 1994). ECPAT began as a sub division of ECTWT (Ecumenical Coalition on Third World Tourism) apparently perceiving child prostitution as an inevitable consequence of foreign tourism (ECTWT, 1990). While such a view may be valid to some extent, it would be too far fetched to attribute the rise in the incidence of child prostitution in India to any single factor, in this case to the so called demand by foreign tourists. Sweeping statement might create unnecessary aversion for all foreign tourists whereas only a microscopic minority among them might be involved. Also such literature totally ignores the presence of local customers who usually are in larger in numbers than foreigners. For example in the Philippines the Japanese are painted as the sole source of trouble for this problem. Similarly number of references are found about Chinese in Thailand. Any researcher need to carefully examine such references.

The problem of commercial sexual exploitation is also referreed to in terms of demand and supply.(Good Shepherd Sisters 1994).But sometime remarks like " Foreign men want children therefore they are supplied " may have long term implications.(O'Grady 1992; 1994;O'Connell Davidson & Brace, 1996). To understand the problem a framework of ideas is necessary. What are the various theories and how does it affect the decision on intervention has been succinctly narrated by Judith Ennew (1996).

Table 2 : **Campaign theories and related theories in the field of the commercial sexual exploitation of children**

Campaign	Theory
Feminism	Patriarchy, the 'girl-child'
Morality	Religion, sexuality, blaming perpetrators,rescuing children
Child survival and Development	Psychology, medicine
International development aid	Poverty, demand and supply(economics), community development
Children's rights (including sexual rights)	Power, childhood, human rights

Adifferent approaches adopted by different groups and researchers we feel that the concept of children's rights alone provides the fulcrum which would help us in understanding the problem of child prostitution.

The `children's rights ' theory is most suitable because it entails discussion on the nature of childhood-what it should be like and how can it be shaped. This theory can be universally applicable because it envisages various sets of relationship involving best interest of the child, the family and the state. In modern governance system the State not only influences the socialisation process of children but also the family's capacity to raise and take care of children. In the era of market economy the best example is that of the parents today in the erstwhile Soviet Union. If we wish to develop a long term vision of better future for vulnerable children in Indian society then we need to measure the contours of development by social justice scale.

Note and References

1. Karl Eric Knutston, `Making Reality of Children's rights', Report of the International Conference on the Rights of the Child, Radda Barnen: Sweden(1989) and personal discussion with the representative of Save the Children International at Geneva, 1992 and 1993.
2. Savitri Goonesekere,(1998) Children.Law and Justice: A South Asian Perspective, Sage Publications, New Delhi

3. IMF Survey, Global Changes Underscore Role of Surveillance,1994,Washington
4. Makrinioti,Dimitra(1994)~Conceptualisation of Childhood in a Welfare State: A Critical Reappraisal." In Qvortrup et al.(1994)
5. Non governmental organisations are being recognized more and more as valuable participants in the implementation of human rights.(CRC/C/20,nr.170)
6. Alston, Philip.(ed),The best interests of the child- Reconciling Culture and Human Rights, Oxford, Clarendonpress, 1994
7. "Sale of children", Report submitted by Vitit Muntarbhorm, Special Rapporteur appointed in accordance with resolution 1990/68 of the Commission on Human rights .United Nations Economic and Social Council, E/CN.4/1991/51,28th January 1991
8. Thomas Hammarberg, note that Article 32 of CRC allows for different minimum ages depending on the nature of the job, states: "The point is that there should be a conscious policy in this field and that children's health and possibilities for education not be undermined." See Hammarberg,T., " The Rights of the Child in Developing Countries: International Norms and Procedures for Real Change?", Human Rights in Developing Countries Year Book 1994
9. UNICEF,(1990) Children and Women in India: A Situation Analysis.Devasia,L.and Devasia.V.V.,(1991) "The Struggle forSurvival of the Girl Child", in Girl Child In India, Ashish Publishing House
10. Karlekar.M(1982) Poverty and Women's Work: A study of Sweeper Women in Delhi, New Delhi, Vikas Publishing House
11. Bruce.F., The Sexual Exploitation of Children,Geneva,BICE,1991
12. UN Commission on Human Rights, Resolution 1994/90,Paragraph 17 entitled "Need to adopt effective measures for the prevention and eradication of the sale of children, child prostitution and child pornography." The Economic and Social Council, in its Resolution 1994/9 authorized the establishment of an open ended working group which met for the first time in Geneva from 14th till 25th Novemb4er 1994.The report of this first session has been adopted by the UN Commission on Human Rights at its fifty-first session(February-march 1995/ Docuemt E/CN.4/1994/WG.14/CRP.3rd-20th December1994)

The author wish to thanks staff of UNICEF Library New York for excellent help and cooperation provided during his visit to the library for references in 1996.

Chapter 3

Theoretical Framework

> "Using children as a cutting edge of human rights generally, our many ongoing efforts in diverse fields of development, would contribute more to international peace and security, and more to democracy ,development and the environment-more to preventing crisis and conflicts - in a shorter period of time at a far lower costs than any other set of doable actions aimed at remedying global problems on the threshold of the 21st century.[1]

As curtain draws on the most exciting century in recorded human history it is time to ponder over the peace and universal egalitarianism that is still our cherished dream. A great deal of scientific and technological progress has been made . But at the same time growing instances of child abuse and neglect are becoming a major problem in many countries. Protection of human life and dignity are care central to the rights perspective.[2] Since the Universal Declaration on Human Rights of 1948, a number of Conventions, Covenants and Agreements have come into effect so far. They stand like lamp posts in the darkness. These instruments would be guiding us to meet the challenges in the new millenium.[3] Some of the international instruments are of our immediate concern.

They include:International Covenant on Economic , Social and Cultural Rights, International Covenant on Civil and Political Rights (1976) International Convention on the Elimination of All Forms of Racial Discrimination ,CEDAW, and the most recent one the

Convention on the Rights of the Child. This is most widely signed and ratified document in the world. There is monitoring mechanism also. Therefore it may provide a reliable tool to check the sexual abuse of children. Article 34 of the CRC explicitly talks about protection from abuse and exploitation. But there are other articles also which need to be kept in mind while monitoring a problem. Our field experience shows that health and education are two important areas which can be of great help in checking the abuse of children.[4]

These elements may not provide a panacea for solving all the problems. But they can certainly help the NGO's, the policy executants and the society at large to monitor the children's welfare, their health and all those aspects that govern their growth and development.

The matrix based on the CRC will help those who are engaged in action programme or even to those who wish to carry out action - research in how to check growing child prostitution.[5]

Table 3: **Framework based on the CRC for measuring and monitoring the child prostitution**

Articles	Ideas
1,2,3,16	Definition of child, children's dignity, non discrimination, respect for privacy
34,35(11,16,17(e)19,32,33,36	Prostitution, traffic, pornography
28,29	Education

It is often argued that measuring the incidence of child prostitution is impossible because of the secretive manner in which the abuse is perpetrated While this may have some truth it should not be a deterrent to carrying out an exercise to determine the extent of the problem. First of all there is a need to go in for a conceptual clarification on child prostitution. Some of the questions one need to address are :What is child prostitution? What kind of children (age, gender, ethnicity) are involved? Who exploits them and in what manner?(Ennew. J., 1996) A collection of micro level data will immensely provide valuable insight into the problem.[6]

Dignity and innocence

Childhood has close relationship with culture. Children grow in certain environment which is influenced by the region's culture. Thus exploration of the meaning of 'culture' must be the basis of any advocacy or monitoring research pertaining to child prostitution. However, the culture should not be allowed to become a tool of exploitation ." Just as culture is not a factor which should be excluded from the human rights equations it must not be accorded the status of a metanorm which trumps rights (Alston.P.,1994). The concept of dignity, innocence and purity affect the thinking of the communities all over the world. The `dignity' concept is fundamental while dealing with the issue. This has been well dealt by a number of anthropologists. Most anthropological writings also agree that cultural notions of honour and shame critically influence and are informed by the constructions of sexuality and sexual morality. The purpose here is not to enter into a debate but to underline the inner currents which influence the thinking. The convention on CRC refers to dignity seven times and it has been claimed that it is concept that permeates the document(Melton,1991). Dignity is referred to in the Universal Declaration of Human Rights also.[7]

In daily life a citizen in his individual capacity may not enter into the philosophical debate over the words referred to in the preceding paragraphs. But what a citizen may look for is easily understandable and life-based experiences to act upon. In this context health and education offers two very visible indicators with which one can proceed to take action in tackling the problem of child prostitution

Health

Gross abuse of children through commercial sexual exploitation can also be perceived as a form of child labour when it results in the exploitation of children for profit.(Savitri Gonashekrhe,1998).Even from this account there are few studies available to gauge the implications on health of prostituted children. Literature available does not speak much of the health and psychological implications of sexually exploited children.

The scope and nature of the health aspects as per WHO are :

* health is a state of complete physical, mental and social well-being and not merely the absence of disease.
* healthy development of the child is of basic importance; the ability to live harmoniously in a changing total environment is essential to such development... (and)
* governments have a responsibility towards the health of their peoples which can be fulfilled only by the provision of adequate health and social measures..." (Preamble of the Constitution of the World Health Organisation)

In order to understand the health implications one can start ;with following primary considerations:

- Define age ranges, related to physical psychological and social development of sexuality as a basic tool for collecting presenting data
- Define cultural understanding of commerce, exploitation exchange and reciprocity in the context of gender custom and sexuality
- Remember that gender and custom and culture are fundamental. To interpret the relevant Articles of the

Convention on the Rights of the Child.

Based on the above understanding some measurable indicators can be fixed.

Although direct scientific data are very limited on the sexual exploitation of children it often results in serious, life-long, even life threatening consequences for the physical, psychological and social health and development of the child. Their future fertility and psychological capacity to establish healthy relationships and their own families is seriously compromised. At the community level the commercial sexual exploitation of children represents an erosion of human values and rights that threatens the health of society. The child's self-protection mechanism is also severely affected but its degree would vary from child to child depending on his/her capacity to bear the trauma of sexual exploitation. The more extreme example of the developmental impact on victimization is seen among those individuals who have physical or intellectual limitations. They are unable to protect themselves and are particularly vulnerable to sexual abuse, and in some instances commercial sexual exploitation. Another group that would seem to be particularly vulnerable to both sexual abuse and exploitation would be girls who become physically mature at a young age but are socially and psychologically immature.

Because child prostitution is illegal and is practised in clandestine manner there has been a paucity of information on its health and developmental implications in the scientific literature. Only recently has there been a critical effort at assessing the methodologies for measuring the magnitude of the problem thus going beyond their routine medical and other check ups required under the criminal and juvenile justice systems. No reliable methods exist for the direct measurement of the magnitude of the effect on the prostituted children But the general reports available indicate that during childhood and the transition to adulthood ,the reproductive system of the girl is particularly vulnerable to infection. The cells and secretion of the physiological immature reproductive tract are too tender as compared to an adult to withstand invasion and damage by sexually transmitted microorganism.[8]

Two of the most common sexually transmitted diseases ,namely C.Trachomatics and human papilloma virus (HPV) infections affect younger people more and the multiplicity of sexual partners makes it more complicated. The early onset of sexual activity greatly increases the immediate and long term consequences of the STDs in young women, pressure of the other STDs also increases the likelihood of HIV infecting individuals adolescent girls. Thus the risk of AIDS increases.

The problems of the prostituted children are mostly seen in the social and economic context and rarely in the context of their needs and vulnerability in attaining developmental health. Only recently health professionals begun to examine risk taking behavior as a public health issue which ,in the past ,have been crisis focused. Pedophiles seek smaller children as their victims. Younger the child less the self-protection capacity.

Pornography

While newspapers, magazines and the electronic media provide episodic and anecdotal accounts of sex rings and pornography, only in the past few years the need for systematic data collection and analysis of the scope and impact of this form of sexual exploitation of children and adolescents has been felt in India. The use of alcohol and drugs, together with promises of extra money for the photographs, plays a key role in enticing the child.

Health Effects

The health aspects of prostituted children should be seen both in terms of the clinical-pathological effects on the individuals as well as the psycho-social and psycho-sexual effects and its impact on public health and social development. The health effects may arise as a consequence of either the direct effects of sexual experiences or the circumstances that have led to the child's sexual exploitation. The effects relate to the consequences of infection, physical violence and/ or sexual abuse, the toxic effects of drug abuse, pregnancy and the psychosocial impact of the experience according to the vulnerability and subsequent expression of psychological, emotional or mental development of the individual.

Direct health consequences

Sexually transmitted infections are the most common direct medical consequences of child prostitution, with HIV/AIDS the most serious of these infections, both for the child and public health. At present at least a dozen different microorganisms have been identified as being sexually transmitted and capable of producing disease in either sexual partner, the fetus or the newborn infant. The effects may either be immediately apparent or delayed and not manifest until years later. In case of infertility the effects are not apparent until failure of a conception in a planned pregnancy. From both the clinical and epidemiological perspective, one of the major problems in making both health authorities and the public to take seriously the problem of sexually transmitted diseases is that in most instances initial infection is either asymptotic or simply associated with local symptoms.

The immediate and long-term consequences of STDs span the clinical spectrum from localized genital tract infection, pelvic inflammatory disease(PID), ectopic pregnancy and infertility in the woman; genital tract, and ophthalmic neonatorum, sepsis and meningo-encephalitis in the infant born of an infected mother.

Pelvic Inflammatory Diseases (PID)is one of the serious consequences of STDs. Infertility is a common consequence of STDs, and is both a consequence of prostitution as well as a factor forcing women into prostitution. Such women - including those married as children, divorced from their husbands and unable to return to their family of origin, frequently turn to prostitution as a means of survival.

HIV / AIDS

Whether prostituted children provide sexual services under an "organized" system or as a consequence of "survival strategy", they are probably at much greater risk of acquiring HIV infection than older individuals in similar circumstances.

First, they are less likely to have been reached with accurate information on the risks and consequences of HIV infection. They are also less likely than older individuals to have access to information on and the means to prevent infection - including condoms, in large part due to their social marginalization. Even if they had such access, their powerlessness -whether due to their exploited position, social or economic circumstances or position of psychological dependence - and lack of skills to negotiate safe sexual practices would nullify the usefulness of the information.

There is already a higher risk of infection in the young adolescent with an immature reproductive tract. Furthermore, due to her age and power relationships, she is less able to negotiate safe sexual practices, once again raising her chances of getting HIV infection. The risk of children becoming infected with HIV may arise from the devastating social and economic consequences of AIDS wiping out or totally incapacitating the adult members of the family, forcing, as in the instance of children into prostitution situations as a means of self and family survival.

Other Sexually Transmitted Diseases And Their Consequences

Besides HIV infection the other three most significant viral sexually transmitted diseases are human papilloma virus (HPV), herpes simplex virus type 2 (HSV-2) and hepatitis B virus. HPV in its acute form causes genital warts, it may cause laryngeal papillomatosis in the infant born of an infected mother, and in its chronic form is among the causes of genital tract cancer. In some settings it is the most common STD among adolescents and is strongly associated with early age of onset of sexual activity and multiplicity of partners.

Psychosocial Consequences

Beside the obvious physical consequences the psychological problems need to be discussed . Few systematic or reasonably controlled studies exist on the psychological consequences among the prostituted children. Furthermore, the extent, depth and permanency of psychosocial damage is likely to have influence on the child in a situation of sex trade.

There are few published reports on specific health care and rehabilitation of victims of prostituted children. Much of what is known in the field has been drawn by analogy from HIV/AIDS control work among commercial sex workers, street children and the principles of community health Programme of voluntary organisations . More often than not the first choice of these children will be in terms of personal security and skills for immediate daily living. While they may seek care for painful conditions and symptomatic illness, once care is provided other immediate needs are likely to take precedence.

On the whole the health system and health workers are ill-prepared to address the health and psychosocial needs of victims of prostituted children. Health workers, being inadequately trained in human sexuality and all of its health and psychosocial dimensions, carry their own biases and judgements when dealing with such problems. Furthermore, public services for health care are rarely designed to take the needs for dignity and confidentiality into account while dealing with prostituted children.

The mapping of the social and judicial responses to prostituted children is an essential component in establishing policies and programmes in preventing further damage to the health and development of its victims and to protect their rights. Such a mapping exercise must include an examination of the systems that deal with the victims like the Juvenile Justice Boards etc.

Education

It is widely acknowledged that without certain basic educational level in the societies economic development alone will not provide sustainable base for human life and dignity. This analogy can be extended to the prostituted children also.

" We must not make the mistake- common in some circles- of taking the growth rate of GNP to be the ultimate test of success and of treating removal of illiteracy ,ill -health and social deprivations- at best- possible means to that hallowed end. The first and the most important aspect of Nehru's listing of what we have to do is to make clear that elimination of illiteracy, ill-health ,and other available deprivations are valuable for their own sake-they are `the task' that we face. (Sen.A., Indian Development, Oxford University Press 1998 page 18).

Education is a vehicle for social transformation and the lack of basic education among females has links with some deep - rooted features of gender relations(Jean Dreze and Haris Gazdar in Indian Development OUP ,1998 page 34). It is here that education provides a tool to the next generation. It inculcates values, attitudes, belief, behaviours and norms. How can education tackle the problem of child prostitution and what role it can play as a preventive strategy ? First, the educational system, working in synergy with other social institutions, can become a proactive force for social change. Second, the educational system can counteract the negative impact and reinforce the empowering and enabling lessons of informal learning. Education is not a panacea, nor will educational measures alone suffice to combat the degradation of children in sex trade. At the same time no, efforts to address the problem will be workable or sustainable without them .In this section an attempt has been made to show that the educational system can and should contribute far more to the solution than it has done so far.

Educational action to combat child prostitution

Commenting on this aspects a document of the Oslo Conference Against Commercial Sexual Exploitation states that," Education, as it best, is an empowerment tool for children, enabling them to develop the necessary confidence ,self-esteem, capacity for reasoning and social skills to protect their rights and dignity and to become productive, fully participating adult members of society. Successful education can also enable adults whose role is to nurture ,care for and educate children to understand and act upon their continuing and changing responsibility in shaping the development of children. And when designed and carried out purposefully, education can create and build the commitment of society as a whole to respect the rights and dignity of its children."

Ratified by as many as 187 states till date, the Convention signifies an almost global commitment to recognize and protect all rights for all children. Now the big question is how to translate them into reality. Most rights of children in commercial sexual exploitation are being breached, the right to education being among them. Could enabling these children to exercise their right to education facilitate their access to other rights? It is possible if educational strategies recognize the principle of indivisibility. Education needs to be accompanied by complementary measures, i.e. legislation, new policies, health programmes, alternative economic opportunities and the commitment to a change in values and attitudes.

An International Commitment

At the World Conference on Education for All held in Jomtien, Thailand, in 1990, the world community pledged to take the necessary steps to achieve primary education for all children by the end of the decade. Jomtien also articulated an "expanded vision" of universal basic education that went beyond access and enrolment to the quality and relevance of learning as a tool for empowerment. The Jomtien goals have become a benchmark for subsequent international expressions of social development goals notably those of the World Summit for Children (1990), the International Conference on Population and Development (1994), the World Summit for Social Development (1995) and the Fourth World Conference on Women (1995).

Commercial sexual exploitation of children is now being placed on the global agenda, and is forging a link with education, for prevention and recovery, is a new endeavour. The World Congress at Stockholm(1996) adopted agenda for action and at the heart of this commitment lies education aimed at changing attitudes and behaviours that will move society irrevocably in the direction of eliminating this horrendous practice.

Given the role of education in promoting social change, what should be its priorities and purposes in relation to combating the commercial sexual exploitation of children? They can be seen from two interlinked perspectives (1) developing the main objectives for designing and implementing educational programmes; and(2) identifying the major categories of learners who must be reached.

In the first instance the efforts should be made to prevent or at least reduce the risk of children falling prey to commercial sex by ensuring their access to and participation in education. Along with this there is a need to support awareness-raising, advocacy and social mobilization among the public at large about the scope, nature and impact of commercial sexual exploitation of children and the need for action.

Among the categories of learners would be children of school age, whether out-of-school, in-school, or currently in the sex trade (and more likely to be out-of-school). The design of programmes should take into account the many relevant differences between boys and girls ; children in rural, urban and varying cultural environments; children who have been coerced and those who have been ushered in the sex industry by their own family members in the name of tradition.

Commercial sexual exploitation of children affects primarily adolescents, a population that usually falls between the cracks of public policies.

To reach all children --those in danger of or are already subjected to the gross violation of rights, two overall approaches are necessary: mainstreaming of measures within general educational programmes for all children;especially-targeted programmes for those who are poorly-served or unreachable by mainstream efforts. Expansion of educational access and participation for all children including potential or actual victims of sexual exploitation and steps to enhance the quality and relevance of educational content.

Children in school are less likely to be exploited than children not in school, although sometimes school children are involved in the sex trade to earn the cash needed for school fees, books and uniforms and transportation. On the whole, participation in primary and secondary education is a means of reducing the vulnerability of children to exploitation and thus a critical part of prevention.

At least 130 million children today do not have access to primary education. Another 100 million do not complete a full cycle. Education beyond the primary level is not generally a part of the universal basic education plan in developing countries, although a majority of the children involved in commercial sex are of school age. According to a UNESCO estimate, close to 300 million adolescents beyond the primary school stage are out of school.(UNESCO, World Education Report, Paris, 1995) Two-thirds of those are girls and a large majority belong to the poor and dis -empowered sectors of society including ethnic and cultural minorities.

Situation in India

Relevantly little is known about the genesis of gender biases in child survival in India. In 1991 ,the death rate in the 0 - 4 age group (per thousand population) was 25.6 for males and 27.5 for females at all India level. The female mortality rate in this age group was lower than the male rate in the southern states of Andhra Pradesh ,Kerala,Tamil Nadu but was higher in all other major states except Assam and Himachal Pradesh.

The literacy rate for female is dismal in India . Almost double for males. For example if 100 girls get education some 201 boys get education. Enrolments of girls of 6-1 1 years is only 68 per cent in the primary level. In group 11-14 year only 29 percent girls attend school as against 54.3 percent boys. In 1981 female literacy rates in rural areas was 17.9 per cent. The general rate in 1981 among Scheduled Castes was 21.3 per cent while it was 10.9 percent among Scheduled Tribes. Literacy rate among the Scheduled Caste women in Bihar was 1.78 per cent M.P. 4.07 Rajasthan 1.08 and U.P. 2.77 per cent in

1981.There female literacy rate among the scheduled tribes in 1981 was 8 per cent while literary rate among ST women was 0.93 per cent in Rajasthan, 2.78 per cent in Andhra Pradesh and 3.91 in M.P. It shows that among the deprived section women and girls suffer more. The SEBC Commission Survey (1976) also found that 68 pert cent of tribal girls in the age group of 7-14 years were illiterate in Gujarat. The tribal areas of Gujarat ,Maharashtra and Rajasthan needs special attention.10 Even the 1991 Census shows 10 per cent increase in overall literacy rate for women, i.e., 39.42 per cent from 29.75 per center in 1981. India has 129 million illiterate women and one cannot help observing that inspite of literacy missions etc. the overall situation is appalling. There is no doubt that the country must give the highest priority to eradication of illiteracy in the shortest possible time.[11]

Even West Bengal literacy rate for tribal women is appalling and shocking ST female literacy only 5 % in 1991 and 22 per cent for SC female.

As per 1991 census only 42 per cent of rural female in 5-9 age group were attending schools. In the 10-14 age group only 32 per cent rural female were attending schools. In U.P. in the 5-9 age group females only 28 per cent and in 10-14 age group only 31 per cent rural female were attending school. It is totally remarkable that in rural India in the 12-14 age group more than quarter boys have never been enrolled in the school and more than half the girls have never seen school. The safety and security of girls and their protection form sexual molestation in school and on the way to school is an issue in many areas of India. Parents often draw great satisfaction in sending their daughters to school if the school has some female teachers. According to Gupta et.la (1993) in rural North India large percentage of parents are hesitant to have their daughters taught by male teacher and this may begin at as early as 7 to 8 years of age.

The persistent gender gap in education both in quantitative and qualitative terms, undoubtedly is linked to the fact that girls comprise the majority of children at risk of and involved in commercial sex. Despite the growing worldwide effort to improve access to education for girls, drop-out rates remain high in many countries and the inequality in attitudes and treatment in the classroom continues. The safety and security of girls and their protection from sexual molestation in school and on their way to school itself is an issue in many countries. The development of a conducive learning environment that ensures retention and completion of girl learners in an educational system, that will enhance their life aspirations, and raise their performance expectations and actual achievement, remains a major problem and a necessary objective. So ensuring participation of adolescents, especially girls, in education remains an important goal. The DPEP can play critical role in this field. There are a number of risk districts in our country and the DPEP could well do a monitoring role and thus help combating child prostitution.

Reaching Outside

While improving access to and quality of education can be a preventive leverage, there is also a great need for schools to address commercial sexual exploitation more directly as it affects the lives of children. The strong resistance of families, teachers and administrators in some places combined with the fact that the majority of children endangered by commercial sexual exploitation are beyond primary school age, makes school outreach-different. Reaching into communities, schools can become effective as a safe and supportive environment in which children and families can explore the sensitive and often taboo subjects of sexuality, HIV/AIDS, unwanted teenage pregnancies, drugs, as well as the development of self and mutual respect and parenting skills for both boys and girls. The urgent need for sexuality and reproductive health education has been expressed by many NGOs and other activists in developing countries; they are also frustrated by the strong resistance to its incorporation in some curricula or extra-curricula school programmes.

The HIV/AIDS crisis has motivated a plethora of programmes in many countries that are school-based, non-academic educational programmes directly applicable to the issue of commercial sexual exploitation of children and excellent models with which to address this issue.

Teachers

In India, a component of the major national UPE initiative, the Teacher Empowerment Project gives teachers decision making powers and creative input in the classroom and encourages them to design and run their training seminars. This strong participation builds teachers' self-confidence and lifts their status in the eyes of the community. It moves them from the periphery into the very centre of the education process. These schools have become child friendly because teachers are using participative student-centered pedagogy and children are involved in song and dance, creating materials, and helping to decorate and maintain classrooms. Parents, villagers and supervisors are now helpers of the teacher and not adversaries who blame them for not doing their job or being unmotivated.

Teachers are often powerful influences in children's lives. At the same time, they can mirror unthinking social attitudes and behaviour and even the most dedicated and committed are often powerless in a system that holds them in low regard. For most work under enormous stress, are poorly paid, lack the support, respect or understanding they are expected to give to children. Even in education reform efforts, teacher education has been largely neglected and only small percentages of financial support have been devoted to pre- or in-service teacher education.

New thinking

India will have to `liberate' itself from its own `past' and reshape educational policies by removing prejudices of class as well as traditional culture. No society can emerge as developed if it merely follows traditionalism. It is absolutely essential to change the way we think. Most social learning is slow and painful but not always. Sometimes we cross a threshold and learning comes about astonishingly swiftly. Who among us would have predicted the sweeping changes in the Soviet Union without firing a shot. When people changed their thinking, the old order simply disappeared. When a society has no. other choice than change, we get little guidance from the past, we cannot predict the future from the past in those circumstances.

The traditionalism ignores the role of growing science and technology and distribution or accessibility to its fruit. Thus sometimes advocating `traditionalism' means implicitly justifying the implications of the social evils, associated with it and depriving poor or traditional people of their rights. For a rights perspective we required a new society based on sustainability. Among other things by sustainable society I mean people care for I`future generations of people too. `The militancy of citizens ' would play crucial role in moving towards such paradigm. If the commercial sexual exploitation of children is ever to be eliminated, even reduced, education must be a true force for change. But education does not work in isolation. An agenda for new millennium would have to be based on comprehensive human rights paradigm. It is in this parameters the health and education aspect need to be seen . So it a political agenda and merely piecemeal cause -effect response will not make dent .Without paying attention to the enabling social changes - in education, healthcare among others - the daughters of mother India would be doomed.

Notes and References

1. Grant James P., Address to the World Conference on Human Rights, Vienna, June 21, 1993.
2. Mishra. Rangnath, former Chief Justice of India and later first chairman of the NHRC in an address to the seminar on Human Rights, New Delhi 10.12.1996. Justice Mishra played very constructive role in setting up the NHRC in India.
3. Bhagwati.P.N., Justice, former Chief Justice of India. He started Public Interest Litigation (PIL) in India. Number of child labour cases were heard in the Apex Court due to him and he gave landmark judgement in bonded labour case.

4. Bellamy,Carol., Statement to the UNICEF -UNESCO, Joint Committee on Education,Paris,May,1996,page3
5. Ennew,Judith., & Miljeteig, Child Watch International Indicators
6. Ibid.
7. Robertsons.A.H.,& Merils J.G.., Human Rights in the World-An Introduction to the Study of the International Protection of Human Rights, New York, Manchester, University Press,1992
8. Mosicki.A.B., et la ., Differences in biological maturity, Journal of Pediatrics,1989 p 487-493
9. Manjoor Ahmed and Sara Ann Friedmam, UNICEF Working Group on Education ,1996,
10.Govt. of India, Women in India-A statistical Profile 1988
11. Bose. Ashish, Population of India, B R Publishing, NewDelhi,1991

Chapter 4

Law and the Prostituted Children

" Salma is dead. I thought I would let you know", a journalist phoned the other day.

Salma, kidnapped slave in fleshmarket, must be 15 at the time of her death. She was nine year old when she was damned.

"Shall I get you bangles of your choice? I had asked her then and lost her friendship. She had looked at me with sharp suspicion. She had jerked away when I had brushed back a strand of hair from her forehead. I realised then that at the age of nine she was terrified of affection. After all her childlike trusting response to amity had killed her.

She, size of a five year old and soft spoken, used to sell biscuits at Pune railway station. A teen age prostitute had sympathetically offered her a trip to Bombay and a movie. From then on it was different story.

Soon she contacted disease. Then a young prostitute brought her to the STD ward of a government hospital, got her admitted and disappeared. A case was registered. After a woman police inspector had recorded the FIR, five male police officers of the Vigilance Branch (VB) had interrogated her and taken down her statement. It was obvious that they were scavenger birds screeching in to grab the spoils by blackmailing the brothel keeper. The brothel keeper would have to pay all five of them to forget that a chick had been trapped and skinned and it had warbled the truth.

Indeed none of the officers followed up the case. The remand home case workers were incompetent worse, they did not bring the investigating officers' apathy to the notice of the juvenile court or the senior police officers.

I discussed these points with the Juvenile Court Magistrate, a woman. She seemed to agree with me on all counts. But she postponed issuance of letter of authority to let me take the child out to the Commissioner of Police, by a fortnight. And then behind my back, she handed over the girl to "her mother" whom sub-inspector, one of the five officers, produced. The VB has an amazing knack of locating mothers of girls whose complete names and addresses are not known. They produce mothers from other states in less time than it takes to travel from the state. Using my judicial permission, I sought to see the court records. They had vanished.

Thousands of little Salmas are trapped and flung before predators. And they die a thousand deaths before they dissipate into dust. When Salma's case was registered, the law was soft. So, I initiated, drafted, pursued and achieved changes in it. The Immoral Traffic Prevention Act was passed in 1986 but I have not heard of a single prosecution of a person who had indulged in commercial sexual exploitation of child with life imprisonment.[1]

The laws are formula in which the social status of a country is summed up, they are its mirror.[2] The Constitution of India has three specific Articles which deal with the children but Article 39 (e) is specific. It says that " the State shall in particular direct its policy towards securing: (e) the health and strength of workers, men and women, and the tender age of children are not abused and that citizens are not forced by economic necessity to enter avocation unsuited to their age or strength. Part (e) says, "The children are given opportunity and facilities to develop in a manner and in conditions of freedom and dignity and that childhood and youth are protected against moral and material abandonment".[3]

The trafficking and sexual abuse of children is prohibited under a number of national laws and international human rights conventions.

International Instruments

Convention on the Suppression of Slave Trade and Slavery,1926. Under this convention, the signatories are to " prevent and suppress the slave trade" and to bring about progressively and as soon as possible the complete abolition of slavery in all its forms." It further puts obligation on the parties to " take all necessary measures to prevent compulsory or forced labour from developing into conditions analogous to slavery.[4]

Forced Labour Convention , 1930

This was one of the earliest efforts by the International Labour Organisation (ILO) which requires signatories to " suppress the issue of forced or compulsory labour in all its forms in the shortest possible period.."

Supplementary Convention on the Abolition of Slavery, 1956

This is an important international instrument as it refers specifically to debt bondage and child servitude as institutions similar to slavery. It directs the signatories to "take all practicable and necessary legislative and other measures to bring about progressively and as soon as possible the complete abolition of debt bondage (and) any institution or practice whereby a child or young person under the age of 18 years, is delivered by either or both of his natural parents or by his guardian to another person, whether for reward or not, with a view to exploitation of the child or young person or of his labour." [5]

International Covenant on Civil and Political Rights (ICCPR), 1966

Article 8 of the ICCPR prohibits slavery and the slave trade in all their forms, servitude and forced compulsory labour. Article 24 entitles all children to "the rights to such measures of protection as are required by his status as a minor on the part of his family, society and the State." [6]

International Covenant on Economic, Social and Cultural Rights (ICESCR), 1966

While Article 7 of the ICESCR indicates that the State Parties shall "recognise the right of every one to the enjoyment of just and favourable conditions of work", Article 10 directs the State Parties to protect "children and young persons from economic and social exploitation."[7]

Convention on the Rights of the Child, 1989

Most widely ratified Convention in the history of UN can be regarded as a historic milestone. It re-emphasises that children too are bearers of all human rights .The Convention is also relevant in the context of child prostitution. With respect to this, articles 19,32,34 and 35 can especially be focused upon.8 In CRC the Articles directly concerned with child prostitution, child pornography and sale of children are articles 34 and 35. Article 34 reads as follows:

State Parties undertake to protect the child from all forms of sexual exploitation and sexual abuse. For these purpose State parties shall in particular take all appropriate national, bilateral and multilateral measures to prevent, '

A: the inducement or coercion of a child to engage in any unlawful sexual activity.

B: the exploitative use of child prostitution or other unlawful sexual activity;

C: the exploitative use of children in pornographic performances and materials.

When we consider this Article it becomes clear that the problems of sale or trafficking are wider in scope than that of sexual exploitation.

Other relevant International Instruments

Sale of children, child prostitution and child pornography have not exclusively been dealt with in the United Nations. Many other institutions and bodies have also taken up these issues.

The Hague Conference on International Private law is an intergovernmental organisation founded in 1893. It deals with the adoption in a focused manner. Adoptions may take place with a view to sexually exploiting the child.

Interpol

Inspired by the remarks made by the President of France when Interpol General Secretariat shifted to Lyons in 1989 a resolution was adopted which stated that the General Secretariat should carry out a study in view of proposed measures to improve international co-operation on offences against minors. Since very little information was available with the Interpol a survey was conducted and based on the replies received form 53 member States, a recommendation was adopted in November 1992.The resolution had three categories. It recommended that national police forces appoint at least one specialist liaison officer whose duties would include: Guaranteeing and protecting the rights and interests of children through the proceedings, and acting as intermediary for the flow of information between various international agencies. It strongly recommended that, `every police officer should receive training in human rights and basic training in dealing with child victims'. Infact, chapter III of this resolution deals with particular problems such as child pornography, child prostitution, sex tourism etc.

Non-governmental Initiatives

The voluntary bodies have played and will play a very important role in raising social awareness. Some international NGOs such as Terre des Hommes, the International Abolitionists Federation, the International Catholic Bureau for Children (ICBC), Save the Children and ECPAT, Defence for Children International and NGO Committee on Child's Rights have taken up the issue of sexual exploitation of children in right earnest.

South Asian Scene

The international legal environment on child rights owes itself much to the developments that have taken place in the Western legal system, in the perception of childhood in Western societies, and in human rights jurisprudence. Critics of the universality of human rights standards (many in South Asia) point out that the origin and content of these standards in international law are clear indication that they are Eurocentric. They are not. The historical evidence of growth and change in Islam, Buddhist and Hindu religious texts suggest that the notion of human rights was not alien to oriental societies. Impact of colonialism on our legal system may give the impression that the concept of human rights has exclusive Eurocentric relevance but in fact they are global in values. (Goonesekere. Savitri,. Child, Law and Justice, Sage, New Delhi 1998. page 17)

All the member States of SAARC adopted a Plan of Action for the SAARC Decade of the Girl Child, 1991 -2000 A.D. The Plan of Action emphasises on the three major goals of Survival, Protection and Development of the Girl Child (Mamta Bannerjee, Minister of State for Women and Child Develoment, 2 Oct, 1992 in National Plan of Action, Govt of India, 1992 Reprint 1996)

This was a conscious attempt to maintain the tempo and the drive of various activities initiated in the region during the Year of the Girl Child. The documents such as Male Declaration of the Ninth SAARC Summit, Male (12-14 May,1991 and Rawalpindi Resolution on the Child (Third SAARC Ministerial Conference on Children of South Asia, Rawalpindi (20-22 August,1996) indicate the need for " stringent measures to protect children from all forms of exploitation" (SAARC SUMMIT 9\11)

In 1997 a SAARC Workshop on Assessment of Problems and Rehabilitation of Children in Difficult Circumstances (26-28 November, 1997) was organised by Dept. of Women and Child Development, Ministry of Human Resource Development which recommended that " there is a need to review and revise all laws pertaining to the children in difficult circumstances in the light of proposed universal definition of the children in the UN Convention'.[9]

Laws in India

There are a number of national laws which refer to the protection of children from exploitation particularly trafficking and sexual abuse. The Suppression of Immoral Traffic Act (SITA), Children (Pledging of Labour) Act are very specific in this regard. Under the Indian Penal Code (IPC) rape, extortion causing grievous hurt, kidnapping, wrongful confinement, buying and disposing of people as slaves are criminal offences. Under the Juvenile Justice Act 1986, cruelty to juveniles is punishable with upto three years' imprisonment and fines.

Article 23 of the Constitution of India says, " Traffic in human beings and beggar and other similar forms of forced labour are prohibited and any contravention of this provision shall be an offence punishable in accordance with the law."

Article 35 empowers Parliament to pass legislation against any action which violates any fundamental right although this right has not been given to the state government. The provision of Immoral Traffic Prevention Act comes under that.

Article 39 prescribes that the state will direct its policy so " (f) that children are given opportunities and facilities to develop in a healthy manner and in conditions of freedom and dignity and that childhood and youth are protected against exploitation and against moral and material abandonment."

Children (Pledging of labour) Act, 1933

Though very rarely referred to, this Act calls for penalties to be levied against any parent middleman or employer involved in making or executing a pledge of a child's labour. Such a pledge is defined as an " agreement, written or oral, express or implied whereby the parent or guardian of a child, in return for any payment or benefit received or to be received by him, undertakes to cause or allow the services that are limited to those made in consideration of reasonable wages and terminable at seven days' or less notice." As per The Children(Pledging of labour) Act

1933 , Sec. 2, "Child is a person less than fifteen years old."[10]

In fact the Act can play a deterrent role. It clearly fixes the responsibility." In this Act unless there is anything repugnant in the subject or context " an agreement to pledge the labour of child means in agreement, written, oral, express or implied, whereby the parent or guardian of child in return for any payment or benefit received by him, undertakes to cause or allow the services of the child to be utilised in any employment.

`Child' means a person who is under the age of fifteen years and `guardian' includes any person having legal custody of or control over the child. Thus the Act provides ample scope to rescue the child from the oldest profession of the world. However, the tendency of the courts to consider home `sacred domain' makes effective provisions ineffective.

Scheduled Caste \ Scheduled Tribes Prevention of Atrocities Act, 1989

This Act covers all kinds of forced labour, including bonded labour or an 'atrocity' if the victim is a member of a scheduled caste or tribe. Committing an atrocity under this Act is punishable with up to five years' imprisonment and fine.

The Suppression of Immoral Traffic Act, 1956 which was amended to the Immoral Traffic Prevention Act makes a distinction between the victims and the offenders and a minimum of seven years imprisonment is meted out to an offender. Previously the Act did not acknowledge the fact that boy children were alsc in prostitution. The amended Act has however acknowledged the fact that there is a significant number of boys in prostitution. (See Appendix 1)

Previously, the Act also did not appreciate the exploitation aspect of the problem and merely the sale of women's sexuality was addressed. Those labelled offenders now include anybody who runs brothels, allows use of premises, lives on the earnings of prostitutes, procures people for the purpose of prostitution, detains in brothels, commits prostitution in public places, seduces or solicits in public places, seduces in custody, does not comply with orders for eviction of brothels, runs correctional institutions without a licence and contravenes any of the rules of this legislation (Joshi, Madhu - 1997; p 39-40). The efficient implementation of these directives is crucial. It is for NGOs to ascertain the effectiveness of the laws and to intimate the government if a hiatus is identified.

Areas of concern

A major loophole in this law is that it fails to take under its purview those who break the law within the family. As is evident from the above, the law restricts the label of offenders to 'public' areas. The family remains immune to the law. In the light of the fact that in many communities it is in fact the families of the women and children who play a crucial role in luring girls into the trade, it is imperative that the role of the family as offender be addressed in the laws pertaining to prostitution.

This household dimension of organised crime should also come under the purview of government policies in general. In fact, from our experience in dealing with the issue of child labour, we feel that this is a classic paradox in defining child labour too. In legal terms, the Child Labour Act of 1986 "allows" by not prohibiting, a child to carry out hazardous work at home although the same may be prohibited outside. The Centre of Concern For Child Labour has been demanding the removal of this lacuna. If the law does not take into account child prostitution and child abuse within the family, at home then it would be difficult to tackle some of the intolerable forms of child labour and child abuse at all. Despite the halo of sanctity around the family, it should be amply clear that child prostitution cannot survive without the support and sanction of the family, Therefore, it is imperative that the law address this lacuna and explicitly define the Constitutional rights and duties of the family.

Annual Reports of the National Human Rights Commission (1995 & 1996) stated that child prostitution and trafficking would be focused in their future work.[11] The Supreme Court of India in its various laudable decisions has taken tough stand on the issue. In its judgement on 10 th December 1996 (M. C. Mehta vs State of Tamil Nadu) the Supreme Court has once again underlined the right to education for all children and protection from exploitation.

New International Initiative

Close on the heels of the World Congress Against Commercial Sexual Exploitation of Children (1996) the recent efforts to bring international check on the growing problem of child prostitution and trafficking of children were initiated by ILO through its proposed new convention on Intolerable Forms of Child Labour. The document by ILO says that `the commercial sexual exploitation of children has in recent years become an issue of global concern , and the indications are that it is on the rise.The root of the commercial sexual exploitation of children in many countries lie in poverty, the inability of rural and urban families to support an educate their children. In some cases ethnic origin, cultural practices and social discrimination render children from indigenous populations, minority groups and the lower castes especially vulnerable. They may not speak the same language, they may not have the right to citizenship and education but once forced into this situation, they are isolated and unable to communicate with the outside world. Commercial sexual exploitation is one of the most brutal forms of violence against child victims.'[12]

Some experts, especially from developing countries have raised the question as to the issue of child prostitution, child pornography and the sale and trafficking of children are on the ILO agenda. It is not child labour. The ILO, "Such repellent abuses are so far removed from any normal notion of work or labour that it seems strange to focus on them in an ILO report. Yet while they are crimes they are also forms of economic exploitation akin to forced labour and slavery." This study is also based on the same principle.13 The tripartite Congress of ILO in June 1998 discussed the new convention and the final discussion will take place in 1999. Earlier an ILO sponsored Amsterdam Conference(26-27, Feb,1997) discussed eliminating the most intolerable forms of child labour including sexual exploitation and hazardous occupations. Speaking at the opening session, the Director -General of the ILO Mr. Michel Hansenne, identified intolerable forms of child labour as:"work in slavery or slave like conditions; in forced labour, in prostitution, in mines, and factories, deep sea fishing and commercial agriculture". He denounced the many million of children employed in such activities as a "variable insult to human rights and an intolerable assault on the dignity of individual." Note the use of the word `dignity' by the Director General of ILO. The use of the word `dignity' conveys his deep sense of commitment towards human rights and the two Covenants, a rare thing in these days of market economy. Yes, dignity is central to human existence. Over 250 delegates from 30 countries participated in this conference.[14]

From time to time researchers and various NGOs have pointed out the enormity of the problem of girl trafficking and sexual abuse. Regrettably, the governments of South Asian region have paid only lip service. For a long time they did not take the reports from NGOs seriously.

However, after the first World Congress against the Commercial Sexual Exploitation of Children (Stockholm, 27-31, August ,1996) the governments which shunned the issue have started listening to the sounds of the footsteps. Save the Children, known world-wide for its work to promote the rights of the children argued during the Congress that," All governments must strengthen legislation against child sexual exploitation and improve the enforcement of existing laws'.[15]

New Law Needed

From the above, it is apparent that the issue of prostituted children in the name of tradition by their own families is still not addressed by Indian laws, and in those cases when the law has indeed been used to protect victims or punish the abusers, the process has been subjective, based mostly on the legal prowess of the lawyer or the sensitivity of the judge. Therefore, a fresh breeze blew when at the suggestion of the NHRC, the National Commission for women recommended that the South Asian Association for Regional Co-operation countries enact a special legislation to tackle the rising flesh trade.[16] "A special legislation is a need of the hour" reads the report of the Goa Conference.It further states, "Simply tinkering with the toothless existing laws is futile. The face of prostitution is changing very fast with liberalisation and globalisation". The special legislation should have provisions for punishing traffickers, pimps (rather than the victims), prohibiting child employment in tourism and hotel industries and banning "traditional" forms of sexual exploitation.

Touchstone of any such new law would be whether it would save another Salma.

Notes and References

1. Sheela Barse, Anatomy of Girl Child (Ed. J A Williams), Asian Youth Centre,1991
2. August Bebel, Women in the Past, Present and Future (Ed. Subrata Mukherjee & Sushila Ramaswamy), Deep and Deep Publications, NewDelhi, 1996.
3. The Constitution of India, Dept. of Law, Govt. of India (as on November 1988).
4. Convention on the Suppression of Slave Trade and Slavery, signed at Geneva, September 25,1926,Protocol Amended the Slavery Convention signed at Geneva, September,1926 with Annex, done at New York December 7,1953.
5. International Labour Organisation, Convention and Recommendations,1919-1966(Geneva,ILO,1966), p891.The ILO also passed the Abolition of Forced Labour Convention (105):India ,however chose not to sign this Convention' (Human rights Watch Children's Rights Project Report ,New York 1996, page 25.
6. International Covenant on Civil and Political Rights, GA Res. 2209(XXI), 21 UNGAOR, Supp.(No 16),UN Doc.63 ,1966, (entered into force march 22,1976
7. International Covenant on Economic, Social and Cultural Rights; GA Res,2200(XXI),21 UN. Doc.A/6316)1966 .(entered into force January 3,1976)
8. Convention on the Rights of the Child GA.Res.44/K5,UN GAOR,44th Session,Supp.No49,UN Doc.A44/736(1989). (entered into force September,2,1990)
9. This author .as one of the resource persons to the South Asian consultation, feels that the stress in this consultation was on practical steps which indicated the willingness of the Gujral Government to move form concern to action.
10. According to R.V.Pillai, the Secretary General of the National Human Rights Commission(NHRC) `age certificate are problem in our country'. Discussion with Mr. Pillai Sept.1997. Shri N.Gopalaswami, the new Secretary General of NHRC, an expert on educational matter, assured this author that the NHRC will pursue to end such 'hideous crimes'.
11. Two members of the NHRC Justice Malimath and Virendra Dayal have played key role in focusing the Government's attention on the issue. Justice

Malimath in his key note address at Goa workshop emphatically drew the attention of the participants to recognise the need for new instruments. National Commission for Women, Report on Goa, National Workshop, on Child Prostitution, New Delhi 1997

12. International Labour Office, Child Labour, Targeting the Intolerqble, 1996, Geneva, Switzerland.
13. This has been the opinion of this writer when he initiated campaign against child labour in hazardous occupations in 1992. In 1994 during Child Labour Action Network's National Consultation at New Delhi this writer argued on the same line but many Indian NGOs find it hard to include commercial sexual exploitation of children's part of `child labour problem'.
14. Amsterdam Conference was addressed by Mr. John Pronk, Minister for Development Co-operation, the Netherlands; Mr. N. Blum, Minister of Labour and Social Affair, Germany; Ms.K.Nordheim-Larsen, Minister of Development Co-operation, Norway; Mr.Arunachalam, Minister of Labour, India Ms. M.Winberg, Minister of Labour, Sweden; Ms.M.Smet, Minister of Labour, Belgium; and Mr. J.J. Notrdman from Switzerland among others.
15. The Stockholm Congress was co-sponsored by the Swedish Government, NICEF, ECPAT("End Child Prostitution in Asian Tourism) and the NGO Group for the Convention on the Rights of the Child. Save the Children is a member of ECPAT and the NGO Group.
16. (Dr. Mrs.Mohini Giri, Chairperson of NCW in a personal interview, Dec.1996, emphasised that `we have been sitting and discussing the problem in conferences and meeting for many years and yet we aren't able to find a solution to the problem. There are several loopholes in the law." Mrs. Jyotsena Chatterji, in a lengthy discussion, Nov,1995 told me that `action by relevant law enforcement machinery' is important. Dr. Jyotsena Chatterjee is Director, Joint Women's Programme and National Networking Committee on the subject is located in her office.

Chapter 5

Selling Fruits of Womb: A Case Study of Rajasthan

I Background

In post Pokhran II India the issues of liberty and social justice are likely to play second fiddle to techno-economic development. The challenges in an inegalitarian society like ours will increase. Therefore, promotion of tolerance, secularism, people's participation in democratic institutions, combating social backwardness and protection of human rights deserve urgent attention.[1] With the rise in aspirations and demand for social justice the conservative elements are falling back on the use of `culture' to keep their control on millions of poor people. `Dignity' of millions has paled into utter insignificance. Though this is an all India phenomenon with the exception of north-eastern region, its manifestation is more visible in certain geographical areas of India referred to as an` area of darkness'. The stark reality feature of the Indian economy is that millions of people live in conditions of appalling deprivation, hunger, ill-health, homelessness, illiteracy and are subject to different forms of class, caste and gender oppression. During the last decade Rajasthan has made progress in the field of industrial development and has attracted considerable foreign investment, yet there is high level of illiteracy, social inequalities and creeping poverty. Though this scenario prevails in all the BIMARU States (Bihar, Madhya Pradesh, Andhra Pradesh, Rajasthan and Uttar Pradesh) the social outcry is found in other areas unlike Rajasthan.[2] the gender disparity is stark in Rajasthan. Bhanvari Devi's case is a classic example.[3] the inner influence of caste in the erstwhile princely states has not changed much. In many areas of the state one feels that `Rajputana' as described by Col. Tod still lives on. Rajasthan has been a cul-de - sae- an area of refuge and isolation in the history of India and from the beginning of the eighth century Rajasthan saw the ushering in of an era of Rajput dominance. With the appearance of the Mughals many changes came in the political and cultural life of Rajasthan. The Rajput -Mughal conflict era is the single most period of medieval history of India which affected the very core of its practices and socialisation process, the prominence of Sati and child marriages are attribute to that. The British dominance started in 1818.

In this chapter we refer to the new economic policies, present state of social development and gender disparity. We have made considerable use of field based observations while referring to the problem of child prostitution. This is an exploratory exercise and further the data is limited. Nevertheless, it does not prevent field-based investigations from providing valuable insights into different aspects of prostituted children in the areas.

Agriculture is not the main economic activity in the state in the sense it is in Uttar Pradesh. Other economic activities are equally important in Rajasthan particularly wool gathering, animal - rearing and stone mining. Rajasthan has a population of 44 million, which is 5.20 per cent of India's total population. Sixty per cent of Rajasthan's 3.42-lakh sq. km area is composed of the Thar desert. Two significant developments after independence need to be kept in mind. First, abolition of Privy Purse and Jagirdari system. Another, adoption of a new employment thrust in mid 80s-employment generation through industrial development, mostly in private sector.

In 1994, the mineral policy was formulated and with it marble and granite stone mining policies were also implemented. The mineral wealth of Rajasthan is well known. In some minerals the state has near monopoly: It produces 100 per cent of the country's wallastonite, 94 per cent gypsum, 75 per cent rock phosphate, 87 per cent soapstone, 90 per cent zinc and copper and has an estimated deposit of 3,000 million tone of lignite. The State has planned to invest Rs. 5,318 crores in power sector in comparison to Rs. 2,352 crores on education during the Ninth Plan period. The industrial sector provides employment to 1.7 lakh and 7.53 lakh people through small and large units respectively. The mineral rich districts are Lakheri, Sawai Madhopur, Udaipur, Pali, Ajmer, Alwar and Banswara. In and around Jaipur gem polishing and precious stone cutting is prominent employment provider industry. The state has a considerable number of cotton textile mills and, cement factories, and of late the state has emerged as major an exporter of granite and marble stones. The state has launched some schemes for employment generation. They are: Udham Protsahan Sansthan (UPS) which was started in 1995-96 to provide marketing support to villages and small scale industries (SSIs) through organisation of State and district level fairs and exhibitions. Women Entrepreneurs Development Cell formed in the Commissionerate of Industries to promote women entrepreneurs and increase employment opportunities. The Indian Institute of Craft and Design was set up to create a new cadre of highly skilled and motivated designers. . The Rajasthan Financial Corporation floated a scheme for financial assistance to 10,000 weavers. An International Trading Zone, Indo-Bazaar, has been created by the RSIDC on the worldwide web where buyers and sellers can converse on a single platform. (Source: based on material supplied by P.N.Bhandari, Principal Secretary Industries, and Government of Rajasthan).

A new tourism promotion scheme was adopted in 1993 and Rural Non-Farm Employment Policy initiated in 1995 in which promotion of tourism is a major thrust area. (Source: Public Relations & Information Department, Government of Rajasthan).

Basic Demographic Indicators

The demographic picture in Rajasthan shows that the female health and survival chances are much lower than the equally poor but more populated state like Uttar Pradesh. Life expectancy is still lower than 55 years and under five mortality is as high as 103. These figures correspond to sub - Saharan Africa. The number of maternal death per 100,000 on live birth in Rajasthan was estimated to be as high as 938 in mid eighties. Only Somalia and Ghana would match them. So far little progress has been made in demographic transition due to a still high fertility rate and low sex ratio rates. In Rajasthan infant mortality rate is six times higher than in Kerala. The life expectancy is 72 years in Kerala.

Table 4: **Comparative figures**

Indicators	Rajasthan	U.P.	India
Life expectancy at Birth			
Male	53.4	54.6	64.2
Female	51.9	56.18	62.3
Crude Death Rate	11.4	12.8	9.6
Rural IMR	103	126	198
Total Fertility Rate	4.7	5.2	3.9
Crude Birth Rate	34.6	37.9	29.9
Sex Ratio	913	879	929
Population ever Married female children (10-14 years)(2)	18.31	11.2	6.59

(Source: All figures are based on census and National Sample Survey quoted in Govt. of India Convention on the Rights of the Child, Country Report 1997, Delhi and Child in India National Institute of Public Cooperation and Child Development, 1994.)

The total health scenario is also not very encouraging in Rajasthan. Even the allotted or budgetary allocations are allowed to lapse. For example under Jawahar Rozgar Yojna Rs.41.60 lakh were provided through supplementary grant in March 1995. Entire amount was returned unutilized (BRS, Health Budget Analysis 1996) In Jaipur district there are 2990 villages but only 604 are covered by village medical facilities indicating that only 20 per cent are receiving Govt. medicare facilities. There is also shortage of trained staff in the Govt. hospitals.

In the health planning and medicare the Block Extension Educator (BEE) has been given important role: organising community meetings, film shows, to reach information education communication. But our field feedback indicates that there is no mechanism at any level of the health system for regular teaching of change in knowledge, attitude,

Table 5 : **Situation of Medical Staff in Rajasthan**

Category	Required	Available	Shortage
Medical Officer	1596	1208	38 %
Male Nurse II	3192	2135	10.5 %
Technicians	1596	1246	30.0%

Source: Field Notes from State Publications, Govt. of Rajasthan, Jaipur, 1997

belief and practices of key directions. So by and large there is no break in trends of improvement in well being, that rates of changes are not very different from countrywide averages and that traditional patterns of deprivation persist and reproduced themselves, particularly in State which has seen some pioneer work by the NGOs in the field of community health and gave the world the Jaipur - Foot. It is said that the river of knowledge Saraswati dried up in Rajasthan some 3000 years ago. The present situation of health reflects the same. The experiments gained by the citizen's initiatives in the field of health seem to have dried up in the corridors of corrupt power-game,

Literacy

Feudal hold and absence of democratic participation may to some extent account for low female literacy rate but this can not be the sole reason because between the period 1981 to 1991 female literacy rate in India went up by 21 per cent whereas in Rajasthan it rose by only 9 per cent. Except in Ajmer region, which was under direct British rule, female literacy and educational efforts remained peripheral in the princely states. Female literacy was recorded 20.4 for Rajasthan (Census Report 1991). In some districts female literacy in rural areas is as low as 6 per cent. The all India average for female literacy is 39.2 per cent.

Rajasthan has the lowest literacy rate among all the states of India (38.6%), barring Bihar (38.5%), while the average national literacy rate is 52.21%. Moreover, while the literacy rate for women in India is a low average of 39.2%, in Rajasthan it is a miserable 20.4%. It is important to note that, the educational level of tribal women is relatively higher in most parts of India than Scheduled Castes and the Muslim minority community. But the table below shows not only gender discrepancies in educational levels but also how low is the educational level of tribal women in Rajasthan which clearly contradicts the overall pattern in India (Educational Survey of India).

The overall literacy rate for Rajasthan is a low 38.6% (20.4% for females and 55% for males). There is a huge discrepancy between literacy rates in the urban (65%) and rural areas (30%) .Of total literate males 41% are found in rural areas and 61 % in urban areas. Similarly of total female literate only 12 per cent are in rural areas and rest are in urban areas. Since the report focuses on certain backward communities a comparative perspective on the literacy rates of population by social groups and gender (as given below) is instructive.

Table 6: **Literacy Rates of Social Groups**

Rajasthan	ST	SC	Other Hindus	Dominant Minority
Male	39%	52%	66%	46%
Female	7.5%	9%	24%	8%
(Source: NCAER/HDI 1994 survey in Sites of Change pp 90)				

This table indicates the striking discrepancies between the rates for men and women across different social groups, the situation being particularly adverse for Scheduled Castes, Scheduled Tribes and the Dominant Minority.

The rates and estimates of child labour in Rajasthan also indicate that exploitation is often worse for the girl child. In 1991 the percentage of children employed for labour was 6%, which is close to the all India average of 6.4%. According to the 1991 Census, in Rajasthan, the position of child labour is far worse for male's (8.2) than for females'

(4.4) in the 5-14 age group category. However the NSS figures for the same are 7.8% for males and 13.5% for females. The higher work participation rates for girl children rather than male children are indicative of the far greater level of exploitation and deprivation among the female child in Rajasthan. In absolute number terms the figures are 417,559 (males) and 677,253 (females) child labourers as estimated by the NSS. It is the NSS estimates that match the visual evidence from field experience.

Table 7: **Literacy rate7yr+(Rajasthan)**

	Male	Female	Total
Rajasthan	55.07	20.84	38.81
Literacy rate Scheduled Caste in rural Areas	20.51	1.81	11.26
Tribal in rural areas	17.88	0.93	9.61
School Dropout rate			
Primary (I-IV)	53.12	60.75	52.25
Middle (V-VII)	62.81	72.82	66.35
(Source: Child In India, NIPCCED, 1994, Educational Survey)			

The per capita budget expenditure (1989-90) in Rajasthan was Rs 132.45 .In U.P. and M.P. the figures were 97.42 and Rs 99.23 respectively.

Table 8: **School drop out rates**

Per capita expenditure		Drop out rates					
		Primary School			Middle		
		Boys	Girls	Total	Boys	Girls	Total
U.P.	Rs. 97.42	47.84	47.24	47.65	49.88	53.34	54.20
M.P.	Rs.99.23	36.64	48.94	41.04	49.88	66.65	55.78
Raj.	Rs.135.45	53.12	60.12	52.25	62.81	76.82	66.35
India	Rs.145.95	43.28	49.42	45.97	58.80	67.80	62.29
(Source: Child In India, Statistical Profile, NIPCCED, 1994.)							

As far as specific linkages are concerned the sobering feature of the educational situation in Rajasthan is persistence of high level of illiteracy among rural females belonging to Scheduled Castes and Scheduled Tribes and high drop - out rates of girls despite incentive schemes. Figurers in Table 1.1 suggest that very high percentage, 18 percent, of girls get married in the age group of 10 -14.This may be the major reason for their drop - out. The illiteracy among female groups in rural areas is another note worthy feature. The districts infected with child prostitution have very low level of literacy among the rural scheduled caste and scheduled tribe female. For instance Alwar-17.53; Dholpur -11.65; Bharatpur-15.53; Dungurpur-12.45; Tonk -12.85 and Udaipur 15.30.In the rural areas and among SC & ST the figure may be as low as less than 1 percent because on the whole female literacy among S.C. is 1.8per cent and among ST only 0.93 per cent. Thus number of schooling years seems to play crucial role and is important linkages to understand ` entry age' of children in prostitution. While mere linking alone is not significant, completing primary and middle school education has linkages with acquiring new skills in non- farm sector of employment and thus may be important while considering rehabilitation strategies

Gender Inequality and Female Deprivation

Endemic illiteracy is not peculiar to Rajasthan's distinct social failure. In fact other north Indian states, U.P., M.P. and Bihar, fare no better than Rajasthan. Even female death rate in rural Rajasthan (in age group below 14 years) which is 11.6 per cent is comparable with number of other backward states. But what is frightening is the death rate in the age group of 0-4 years. This is 41.3 per cent of all death under 14. And it is almost identical for rural and urban areas indicating heavy biases and ` unwelcome' attitude towards the female child. The son preference seems to be higher than other states in Rajasthan. In Rajasthan it is very common to hear," Through the sons one conquers the world, through the grandson one obtains immortality, and through the sons grandsons one attains the region of sun " (Manu Smiriti Vol. V Verse 137,Dr. Jha's Translation). The institution of sonship is considered to be extremely important in

Rajasthan. Son is called `put' in Sanskrit the world putra is derived from the word `put' which means hell and therefore son is the one who redeems his father from the hell. This may also result in low status of girl child.

There are two notable schemes in the field of education: Lok Jumbish and Siksha Karmi. They achieved some remarkable results. The scope of this research is not to examine the effectiveness of these projects. But just to point out that despite such laudable effort s Rajasthan still has very low level of elementary school participation - more than 75 % of 6-10 years old girls and 90 % of 11-13 year old girls in rural areas are not in schools. (Gender and Poverty in India, The World Bank Report 1991) The general efforts in the field of education seem to have done little effect as far as the general education is concerned. The disadvantageous effects of being female seem to be quiet widespread syndrome in Rajasthan.

Question of Poverty

Well argued discourses are available which point out that female illiteracy affects child survival and literacy creates knowledge base for social change. (Jain, 1985; Beenstock and Sturdy -1990; United Nations -1993; Dasgupta -1993. and most notable Dreze.Jean. and Sen Amratya, 1995)

High incidence of poverty in Rajasthan as in other northern states makes Rajasthan no special in this field but in Rajasthan geographical conditions affect poverty alleviation Programme to a large extent. But poverty alone can not be cited as reason for the current level of gender disparities that exist in Rajasthan. With little access to education and health women in Rajasthan are still struggling for survival. This is also evident from the fact that though the nursing profession is normally considered to be female domain throughout South Asia, male nurses in Rajasthan dominate it. In case of Rajasthan despite per capita budget expenditure being more than M.P. and U.P. the literacy rate is lower and drop - out rate higher. Another factor, which deserves attention, is prevalence of early marriages. There is no organised political will to spread female illiteracy in Rajasthan. For instance despite a dismal picture of even primary education for female, particularly the rural female the recent efforts in Rajasthan were made only for floating degree colleges i.e. higher education. (Some 21 colleges have been opened in Rajasthan during the last 7 years. (Source: Director, Public Information, Government of Rajasthan, September, 1998 release). Here we need to understand that educational programmes need support from the state and the society as well.

The indifference and apathy in Rajasthan towards female problems also get reflected in the actions of Government of Rajasthan and policies pursued in the field of women's development. The Government of Rajasthan launched a women's Development Programme (WDP0) in 1984.The articulated objective of the WDP was to empower women through communication, information, education and training and to enable them to recognize and improve their social and economic status (Govt. of Raj, 1984). Under the WDP, a number of Sathin (village level women workers) were appointed whose responsibilities included arming women groups to raise the issue of alcoholism among men, creating awareness against dowry, stopping child marriages and harassment of women. Formation of village level women groups was key strategy. In 1994 a Sathin (Bhanvari Devi) was gangraped for stopping a child marriage of an upper caste Hindu. She herself was from lower caste Hindu background. This issue was taken up by a number of women groups including National Commission for Women and Bhanvari Devi even went to Beijing to attend World Conference on Women. But the end result has been that the Government scrapped the Sathin scheme despite valiant protests by women groups all over the world. The total dependency on state apparatus for social reform without mass base can end up in frustration and setback. Any state committed to social justice has to go beyond welfare measures in order to secure good life for the downtrodden. The human rights approach thus becomes fulcrum of social change.

On employment front the work participation rate of women is very low. And the wage structure in agriculture is also exploitative in Rajasthan.

It was reported to be Rs.12.43 for male and Rs.7.63 for female in 1984. The distribution of female non agriculture and own account workers by regions and State shows that Rajasthan has only 2 per cent where as Andhra has 16 per cent, Madhya Pradesh 11 per cent and Orissa 7 per cent. The analysis shows that women working in non- - agriculture own account enterprise are heavily concentrated in the South. The three states, Andhra, Karnataka and Tamil Nadu nearly account for 44 per cent of all Indian women workers in this category.(see table 5.6)

Other factors also indicate the particularly low status of women in this belt. The percentage of women who are employed is increasing but one needs to delve a little deeper to realise that the real index of empowerment i.e.. What percentages of women are doing what is termed, as 'main work' in the Census is still very low for women? In Rajasthan, females account for 19% of the 'main work' done, while men do 80% of it. Moreover, even within this, for every rupee that the male worker is paid, the female worker is paid 84 paise on an average. (Rao, Rurup and Sudarshan, Sites of Change, 1996)

The " Pink Triangle"

In tourist jargon the Agra-Delhi-Jaipur belt is known as the 'golden triangle'. What is a gold mine in terms of tourism is wreaking havoc with women and children in the area, which covers parts of the states of Uttar Pradesh, Rajasthan and Madhya Pradesh. For the pedophiles the area is Pink Triangle. It is spread in about five districts and is located between Agra-Jaipur-Gwalior. Dhaulpur, Alwar, Tonk, Morena are some of the welknown areas where prostitution is `family occupation' among certain communities. Apart from the festivals, art and culture of Rajasthan that encourage tourism, the Alwar-Jaipur belt also has the Sariska tiger sanctuary. It adjoins the Bharatpur district, which is famous for its bird sanctuary, which draws huge crowds seasonally. Rajasthan earns a substantial part of its revenue from the tourism industry.

The fact that there is blatant trafficking in women and children in this

Table:9 **Distribution of Female Non-Agricultural & Own - Account Workers, by Region & State**

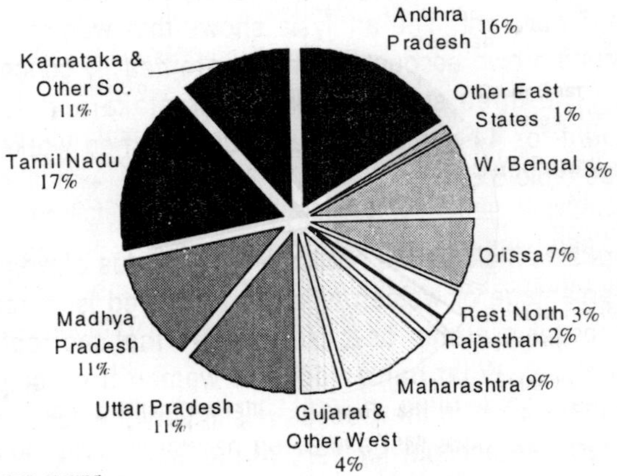

Source:NSS. 38th Round

triangle was most clearly brought out by a journalist who posed as a customer and bought a woman for less than 2000 rupees in Dholpur district of Rajasthan, as one would buy any other commodity. Moreover it is reported that there are annual fairs in and around Dholpur district where women and female children are sold. Added to this is the visible profusion of sex-shops along the highway.

This triangle includes within its ambit the Agra-Jaipur highway, which covers the Alwar and Bharatpur districts of Rajasthan. Alwar town happens to be the centre of truck operators in the western belt of India. An estimated 1500 trucks pass through Alwar town every day. Another 2000 or more trucks pass through Jaipur town. The truck drivers take their breaks at 'dhabas' and sex shops operate in nearby areas. This has given considerable impetus to the flesh trade in the area.

One very significant cause behind the growth of unabashed trafficking is the very low status accorded to women in this region. The situation is particularly bad in the agricultural sector (although less hazardous), mining, quarrying, household industry and manufacturing other than household industry. In and around the urban and suburban areas of Jaipur there are flourishing carpet weaving, gem polishing and mining industries which employ a huge number of children and contribute to enhancing the attitude that it is all right to exploit women and children, it is all right to deny children their childhood and it is all right to pay women and children less than the minimum wage.

The sex ratio is another index of the adverse situation for women in Rajasthan. While the sex ratio in India is 927 female per 1,000 male, which is shocking in it, this figure is 910 in Rajasthan. Again Rajasthan ranks amongst the three worst (states for infant mortality - (53%). To add to this, there is considerable violence against women in Rajasthan ranging from incidences of child marriages, dowry deaths, bride burning and Sati.

The preference for a male child is inscribed in many of the customs of Rajasthan. A man left without a male issue is almost obliged to adopt a son. Even if she is the only child, a girl child cannot under any circumstances inherit the father's property the father passes on his property to the adopted male child.

A woman's status is in these communities defined via her husband, and her son. Interestingly, despite this general preference for the male child in Rajasthan, the communities surveyed - Badiya, Kanjar and Raj Nats- have a marked preference for females. This drastic reversal of trend is because of the fact that the main source of livelihood of these communities now is woman and trafficking in the girl child. And our study confirmed earlier reports that the incidence of atrocity, violence and exploitation towards the vulnerable sections of society is on the increase in this area.

The striking thing is that in Rajasthan in particular (though the situation is not dissimilar in the rest of India) the attitude is such that this is considered the normal state for women to be in. It is widely believed that women are meant for undertaking hazardous jobs. This being the accepted attitude it is not surprising that the status of the woman in this area remains wretched right through her life and she is seldom given the option to improve it - the word 'choice' is not a part of the Rajasthani women's vocabulary. In fact, perhaps the justification for sending a girl child of 11 or 12 years to prostitution is because of the fact that a girl child is married at this age. So there is nothing wrong, the guardians of the prostitutes maintain, with child prostitution. It may be noted that both contravene the law of the land, but in Rajasthan, so far as child marriage is concerned, the law enforcing agencies turn their face.

`TEGs ' - historical factors

In certain districts including the Alwar-Jaipur belt there are some nomadic/semi-nomadic communities such as the Bediya, Kanjar and Raj Nats which have induced their daughters and women to enter the flesh trade. There are historical reasons for such an occupation being the only source of livelihood not just for the girl / woman but also for the families and the community itself. These communities have some common characteristics. Many of them were accomplices in the 1857 mutiny against the British Raj. They aided in supplying materials to the mutineers and so on. Thereafter, it is believed, the British looked upon them as a community specializing in criminal activities. So they came down heavily on them. Subsequently, these communities had to take to other occupations and in the absence of any other options they began to send their women and girls in the flesh trade. These communities were traditionally entertainers; they performed at ceremonies held by the rich in the village. The most auspicious occasions like marriage and birth of children were thus desecrated by this denigration of women and girl children. These women were also used for sexual pleasure of the rich; they however, did not take to prostitution as such. There is evidence to suggest that these groups spread in central and western India, mostly in princely kingdoms outside the direct supervision of the Mughal rules. They moved around in groups of three or four families, singing, dancing and telling stories from the great Hindu epics of the Mahabharata and the Ramayana. They were supported by rulers and to a lesser extent by big landlords. Their patrons and clients provided them with their basic needs and in return these communities entertained them and provided them with sex.

In modern times with the onslaught of radio and films demand for singing and dancing declined. With the abolition of Zamindari, patrons could not support them and the women from these traditional entertainment groups (TEGs) took to prostitution, and the menfolk started justifying it in the name of `traditions'.

'Providing entertainment' soon acquired broader connotation. It implied sex that became part of their job. Women of these communities who entertain were not allowed to marry or do anything else for an occupation although the situation has changed now. With the trade becoming very lucrative, the perpetrators seek to justify this practice in religious and cultural terms. This is precisely where the middleman became important. It is the middleman who usually ensures that the young girl is given grooming and maintained till the time she is inducted into the profession. The middlemen have cold bloodedly created an incredibly organised network for the perpetuation of this hideous evil.

While poverty clearly emerges as the immediate cause behind the practice it is not the driving force that sustains it. It is the middleman's exploitation of a cultural belief, which is sustaining the practice and accounts for its spread. It is, therefore, in the middleman's best interest to keep the trade away from the scrutiny of concerned citizens for he/she stands to gain the most from such a trade.The tragedy is that the middlemen are all too often family members controlled by well-organised groups usually living in big cities. They are powerful protectors of `TEG sex trade' who are often very difficult to identify.

There are a number of reports indicating the increase of women in prostitution. Newspaper reports document from time to time, the mushrooming of highway sex shops on the Agra-Jaipur road. The women are by and large from the Bediya and Raj Nats communities. They stay with their families who are instrumental in socialising with the girls and making them believe that this is their only future occupation. The flesh trade therefore, swallows the girl who grows up in this environment at a very tender age. Despite the pervasive nature of the problem hardly any serious study has been done on the girl child in these communities and on the moulded and manipulated psyche and future of girl children whose mothers practice prostitution.

Perspective and Material

The objective of this study is to trace and analyze the life pattern of prostituted girl children in TEGs, starting with their family background, educational aspirations and onto the possible occupational mobility. We wanted to explore the reality behind the cultural guise for this practice. However, our main concern has been to explore with a view to helping policy makers to design intelligent and holistic development programmes for those sections of society that need such aid. In this regard it is really the manipulated psyche and future of the girl child that we seek to reveal. Only a development programme, which appreciates her predicament and moulded mind, would be capable of addressing the issue efficiently and compassionately. It is in this regard that our micro-level efforts have relevance at the national level.

Processes such as commercialization, population growth, technological innovations etc. are affecting the quality of life of poor people (Gough and Shama, 1973). Rajasthan has been chosen as our research area because problems of low status of women and high incidences of violence against women. In number of cases in which bonded labourers were rescued in other parts of country many of them were reported to be from Rajasthan (Anti Slavery Society reports, 1993)

Then came the incidence of Bhanvari Devi, a village level social worker (Sathin) who was raped for stopping a child marriage in her village. While this was motivating factor for us to undertake this study, the driving force was our exposure to the issue during Social Summit in Copenhagen and preparatory meetings in which issue of girl child was raised by our organisation, Centre of Concern for Child Labour.

We faced the problem of how to study a group that lives in seclusion. So the first question was:

Which strategies do the TEGs use to survive?

On the basis of the literature, studies and observations we hypothesized that the TEGs are using four important types of survival strategies that can be distinguished in relation to labour (Rothschild, 1980 McGee 1979).

(a) The multiple earning strategy: In this all members of the family have to work in order to earn access to entitlement to basic needs.

(b) Child labour: The full exploitation of the child labour force by parents.

(c) Flexibility in size and composition by reducing \enlarging the group by getting members from other relatives such as young girls, boys, sisters, brothers etc.

(d) Migrant labour: sending out members of the household to search for work in different places because they cannot find enough income form the local market.

There is no doubt that for the TEGs the multiple earning strategy is most important. But property and power are practically non- - existent among the TEGs; so making living and striving after the multiple earning depends wholly on the wage labour opportunity assigned by society to the several members. But we notice that due to historical factor this has been greatly restrictive and today only women and child labour in their household are able to earn something.

The next question to be asked in view of the major objectives of the research is:

What are the impact of modernization and other process of social change?

For an answer to this question we have to investigate what direction this impact takes. In this era of overall decrease in labour and income opportunities how is it going to affect the TEGs.

Secondly what is the sexual division of labour between women and men. The majority of women and girls work as `prostitute' and men act as pimp.

Many women studies indicate that among the poor, the women are most disadvantaged even when development has taken place. Use of `culture' or `tradition' to exploit the poor and illiterate is visible in India and a number of studies have pointed out this. Therefore, our third question was:

Do the girls in TEGs communities have any opportunity for acquiring education and skills so that they can exercise or choose alternative way of life? Or in other words what are the possibilities of rehabilitation schemes and of what kind.

To understand this question, we directed our attention to the concept of childhood among TEGs and awareness of HIV \AIDS.

These are all crucial questions. Since women are the mains `breadwinner' in the household an effort to view men's work in context of women is also important. Our finding, contrary to general notion, pointed out that men in TEGs have been marginalised in the process of change and that has resulted in their `deviant' behaviour. Thus forced by the survival urge the TEG households find nothing wrong in ushering their girls into prostitution. We think it is important for men and women to improve their fate 'but the germ of emancipation can only develop and bloom when certain opportunities of survival are guaranteed".

Source Material

The material consisted of structured and informal interviews, life histories, census data and observations. The study is of an exploratory nature. Villages were chosen based on the guidance and help given by the villagers who pointed out the places that had traditional communities engaging in sex trade. These villages were mainly near the highways making their services accessible to the travellers and truck drivers who frequent the area.

Having first identified the problem, preliminary discussions were carried out to prepare a structured questionnaire for interviewing the prostituted children. Samples of 200 girl children were interviewed from various villages in the two districts of Jaipur and Alwar. Knowledge about the families of these girls was itself crucial to what we were seeking. The field workers first established a rapport with the elderly women in the community who were no longer in the profession and were helpless. Their predicament made the need for rehabilitation very clear. It was through them that we gained access to the communities. Our study is based on talks and purposeful discussion with TEGs community leaders, local people, with officials of the welfare department and others.

The total time spent in the field was between July '95 and February '96 although contacts were maintained even after the study was over. The first contacts with village and family elders took at least 2-3 weeks to establish and it took another 2-3 weeks to establish a rapport to enable them to share information about a sensitive topic such as this. The questionnaires were not filled up in front of those who were interviewed and this prolonged the period of study. Special efforts were made to win the confidence of the dejected, elderly ladies in the village who no longer have 'market value' in the trade and could do nothing else to make a living. There were two villages where the elderly women were particularly helpful in giving us the insight that only a victim can provide. The information provided by these women was of great help to us.

The study has some limitations. Our choice of villages was restricted by their accessibility. We were unable to gain any information about child prostitution in any other community. While collecting the data for this study we also faced a great deal of resistance from some of the middlemen. This was a direct result of a rumour that was spread that the families involved would be evicted if their reference came in the record. Information about the movements of girls or women in the trade was severely restricted because it was a closely guarded secret. No outsider was told anything. The secrecy was all the more impenetrable because the clusters were in habitated by single communities and marked by for homogeneity and unity. Besides, only a few men and women knew the inside information. Children were interviewed in their own premises in the presence of people watching over. This presence might have influenced their answers.

The study is from human rights point of view. The idea of the study was to identify the nature of the problem and bring its content to the notice of the government, UNICEF, NHRC, NCW, NGOs, victims and perpetrators, researchers and the public at large.

AREA PROFILE

Alwar and Jaipur districts are the focus of this report. According to the 1991 Census the population of Alwar district is 2,286,701 with a sex ratio of 889 females per 1000 males. The population of Jaipur district is 2,722,551 with a sex ratio of 890 females per 1000 males. These two districts are the most populated districts in Rajasthan because of the industry and tourism incentives. There is nonetheless still a large rural population in both the districts. The main occupation in the rural areas is agriculture but due to the seasonal nature of this occupation there is a high incidence of migration to the urban areas within and outside the districts.

Locating villages where women and children are taking to prostitution for cultural reasons was a difficult task. Some of these villages are located in Alwar district and some in Jaipur district. On the basis of prolonged dialogue and information elicited from the local people, it was found that there are about 40 villages, each having a 'dhani', where prostitution is taking place on a large scale and girls as young as 14-15 years of age are seen to be soliciting customers. ('Dhani' is a separately marked place in a village corner meant for use for prostitution).

A total of eight village clusters in Alwar district and four in Jaipur district were surveyed. In Alwar district the villages surveyed were as follows: 1. Kalsada 2. Basti Gazuki 3.Griwas 4. Sodabans 5. Ullahadi 6. Munni Bai ka Bagh (modern syntax)7. Ramgarh 8. Lawa-ka-vas.In Jaipur district the villages surveyed were 1. Nandlalpura 2. Harsulia 3. Bhojpura 4. Teelawara 5. Hingonia . The number of households differed in each village cluster or highway settlement.

All the clusters put together would have an approximate of 1900 households and a population of about 5,500.` The majority of the populations in these clusters are Raj Nats, Badiyas or Kanjars. One community inhabited each cluster or settlement only.

Topographically, the village clusters of these families are in low yield agricultural land area.The better standard of living for these communities in comparison to the other people in the village suggests that there are `other' sources of income. The area's main agricultural yield consists of maize, potatoes and linseed oil.The people have no other means of earning their living unless they make seasonal migration part and parcel of their life style.The option for these people stricken by poverty is either to migrate to towns and work as construction workers under extremely hard and exploitative conditions or to send their women to the brothels of Bombay, Surat, Agra, Baroda to supplement their income.

II OBSERVATIONS IN THE FIELD

The study conducted in the villages around Alwar revealed that many of these women and adolescent girls were taken for prostitution to places as distant as Bombay and even the Gulf countries. Based on the information of local social workers and other concerned citizens, it is evident that the incidence of sex trade in the area has increased in the last five years. But owing to the illicit nature of the activity not many are willing to share information about the movements of these 'fallen' women.

Women's honour is supposed to be sacrosanct in India and protected by family members in India. But in these communities it was found that not only were the women disrespected but also even harassed by their own brothers, fathers and boy friends that are parasites on the incomes of the women. The career of a girl in prostitution follows a set path. A good looking girl is inducted into the trade early in life; if she is particularly good looking, talented and has family members who are hungry for a better income she is sent to Bombay or even to the Gulf for better 'opportunities'. Girls are groomed to be artful sex workers. The girls who go to Bombay or the Gulf have houses with corrugated roofs, grills, windowpanes, TV sets and coolers. The looks of the houses where prostitution takes place are therefore considerably better. The houses often have more than one tape recorder, pressure cookers, steel utensils and so on.

The life style of men folk in these communities is very different. We observed that the men of these households spend their time lying around on 'charpais' under the shade of trees and playing cards. But all the while they keep a hawk's eye so as not to let a traveller or a truck driver go by unsolicited by one of their women.

The men leading a kind of a life style distinct from others in the village are subjects of discussion, because of the profession their women are in. When the men were asked to account for the anomaly of prosperity despite the hard conditions they pointed to the houses that are involved in sending their daughters out. Those in the village, who have not yet been 'fortunate' enough, aspire to send their daughters as soon as possible so that they too might improve their living conditions and standards.

In one cluster, we found that about 70% of the girls aged between 16-18 have been in the flesh trade in their village already for three to four years. This does indicate the early induction of the girls. Young College boys and the nouveau-rich class come to these clusters in their Maruti vans to take girls aged 13 and 14 years out for 'disco dancing'.

Do people object to the cluster of families traditionally practising prostitution? This question was posed to two categories of people. One was the inhabitant of the cluster within which the trade is practised and the other was the inhabitant of the villages adjoining these clusters. In the villages, a few had outright objections to the presence of clusters where prostitution is rampant. The majorities were silent and their silence spoke volumes about their fear of the police, among other authorities, which are hand in glove with the middlemen.

In Chowki bas and Ramgarh the incidence of prostitution seems to be particularly high. This cluster has about 200 households and a population of about 1600. The 'dalals' are concentrated on the main road. According to some social workers, many households secretly send their daughters of between 12-15 years of age to Bombay to learn how to 'disco dance'. These respondents also said that the young girls on their return to their home villages serve as examples of prosperity, and therefore also encourage the practice of this profession in more commercially lucrative zones. The Bombay-returned girls in fashionable clothes, their make - up with foreign cosmetics and the money they bring, lure other village bellies into the trade.

Information given during the interviews confirmed that it was all an open affair. Among Badiya households it is astonishing that despite SITA (Suppression of Immoral Traffic Act) roadside sex shops operate which can be seen along highways although their exterior often resembles a 'dhaba'. Either out of fear or due to economic want, the people from the village have no objection to the phenomenon and its persistent spread and increase. Their attitude may also be one of resignation in the face of the indifference of the administrative authorities. Whatever may be the cause for this collective silence it is child prostitution which is increasing at an alarming rate and deserves serious attention from policy-makers, law enforcement agencies and NGOs.

Despite State government development measures like setting up `aanganwaris` and 'balwaris' in the area; few of these village development programmes have reached the families practising prostitution in this area. The much-acclaimed 'Sathin' project has hardly made an impression in the cluster inhabited by the Badiyas, Raj Nats and Kanjars. (The present government has discontinued the Sathin Programme).

In two villages of Jaipur district, child prostitution was found in Nandpura Mahla and Bhojpur (Madhopur) in Fagi tehsil. The total number of households practising prostitution is about 125 and the population is about 500. While doing the survey, 70% of the households were visited and its members were interviewed. In some households it was found that a few girls were being sent to school. However, one villager said that the presence of the 'dalals' in the area who had contacts in Jaipur City saw to it that the girls were withdrawn from the school. This affirms the fact that prostitution continues to intensify despite educational opportunities perhaps because the women of these communities cannot resist the hold of the parasitic men of their community.

The literacy rate among the traditional families practising prostitution in Jaipur district is a little better than the rate in Alwar district. Also most girls between the age's 10-14 years expressed the desire to pursue studies or pick up some skills. There was one girl amongst those spoken to who had high aspirations of becoming a teacher. There are primary schools in most of the villages but they are not accessible to children of these communities.

Most of the households were involved in prostitution but no one was willing to talk. It was only after a great deal of persuasion that some of the people agreed to talk. The NGOs doing development work hardly address this question. Here too, the women have not heard of the 'Sathin' Programme. If the local administration had helped the large number of development programmes under way in Rajasthan, awareness about child prostitution would have been greater and the communities practising it would be more aware of the hazards it involves. This itself would have gone a long way in checking the growth of child prostitution in the area.

The study covered 200 girl children belonging to women in prostitution - 100 from Jaipur district (Harsulia - 40; Nandpura - 40; and Bhojpur - 20), 100 girls from Alwar district (Kalsada - 10; Chowki-ki-bas, Ramgarh - 10; Soda Bas Nadi - 10; Lavaka bas - 10 and Guju ki Nadi - 50). The age group was 10-18 years.

Although the tables below record the responses of the 200 girl children of women in prostitution in the areas listed above we held discussions with the elders of their families also. While the responses of the elders have not been tabulated, in the explanation accompanying some of the tables some of the responses of the parents have also been included.

Table 10: **Age wise distribution**

Age group	Number of respondents	Percentage
10-14	133	66.3
15-16	47	23.5
17-18	20	10.2
TOTAL	200	100%

Out of the 200 circumstantially selected respondents, a large number of girls were in the age group category of 10-14. In the entire area studied, the total number of girl children of women in prostitution under the age of 18 was 1500. Again in this group the largest number of girls are found in the 10-14-age category. The great decline in number of girls of the ages of 17 and 18 was explained to us by saying that they had married and migrated out of the natal villages.

One question posed to the girls was at what age they had joined the trade. Many of the girls in the 10-14 category said that they had joined the family tradition 'parivarik dhanda' before they attained the age of 14. The girls of the age categories of 15-16 and 17-18 confirmed this also. A majority of these girls said that it had been 5-6 years since they had first taken up the trade. On the whole 64% of the girls admitted to having been used for purposes of commercial sex before the age of 14.

Table 11: **Reasons for girl children prostitution**

Variable	No. of Respondents	Percentage
No option	124	62
Monetary need	38	19
Induced	17	8.5
Volition	12	6
No response	9	4.5
TOTAL	200	100%

When asked for the reasons for adopting the 'parivarik dhanda' at an early age 62% said they had no option and 19% said it was monetary need that compelled them. However the girls responded in such routine manner that there is scope for doubt.

Table 12: **Awareness of the illegality of child prostitution**

Response	No. Of Respondents	Percentage
Yes	50	25
No	83	41.5
No response	67	33.5
TOTAL	200	100%

With regard to the illegality of the use of children for commercial sexual purposes there were mixed reactions. Only 23% of the parents of the respondents said that they knew that what they were doing was not legally allowed. The majority of the girls and their parents said that it was not illegal but the parents added that they could do as they please with their daughters. And 33.5% chose to make no comment on the matter. This makes a clear case for making the people aware of the legal provisions against such practices.

Table 13: **Respondents' suggestions to stop child prostitution**

Variables	No. Of Respondents	Percentage
Residential care for girl Children upto 18 years	78	39
Involvement in income Generating activities	89	44.5
Female education	13	6.5
Reform the Legislation	6	3
Strengthen the administration	14	7
TOTAL	200	100%

* The 'ashram' type of institution away from the influences of the mother's village where the children could permanently stay, work and educate themselves and be visited by the mothers whenever convenient.

When asked for suggestions to help the situation and save the childhood of girl children in prostitution, 44.5% of the girls said that income generating activities would greatly benefit the girls so that they could have alternatives to earn and run the household independently. Provision for residential care for girls, along with education and skill-training facilities was the next suggestion. Only 7% felt that strengthening the administration would be of any help. It was the 17-18 age group category who looked towards reforming the legislation to improve the situation.

Table14: **Education level among girls**

Age group	10-14	15-16	17-18
Primary	13	3	-
5th - 8th	4	2	-
Above 8th	5	-	-
Total number ever enrolled (including drop outs) :	40/133	7/47	4/21
Total number of respondents who want to either go back to school or want some kind of an education:	21/133	10/47	1/21

Inquiries about the education level indicated that a mere 25.5% of girls in all the age groups put together were enrolled in a school and continued for hardly two years. About 75% therefore never went to any school. However, among those never enrolled in the 10-14 age group 16% of the girls expressed a desire to attend school or educate themselves through some non- formal means.

The trend that emerged during our survey was an affirmation of growing interest in education in the last 5 years in these communities. Most of the respondents in the 10-14 said that they had some primary education whereas the percentage of girls enrolled in the group of 17-18 was very low. So the need for education is being appreciated. It is essential that this interest is provided with an outlet for expression and this would require government and voluntary agencies to step in and make provisions for the education of these children. Regular schools are just not conducive for study because the girls are shunned since they are the children of prostitutes.

Table 15 **Girls' opinion on preference of type of skill training**

Age group	10-14	14-16	17-18
Tailoring	10	7	1
Modern Dance	30	23	14
Music	15	5	1
Beautician	18	1	-
Electrical Repair etc.	2	1	-
Any other	2	-	-
No response	56	10	5
TOTAL	133	47	21

With regard to skill training, the blinker and moulded psyche of the girls clearly comes through since about 33.5% of all the girls expressed a desire to learn 'modern dance' which could be directly related to the profession of their mothers and older sisters or girls in the village. The absence of any other kind of role models has clearly taken its toll on these girls.

Table 16: **Specification of Habits**

Age group	10-14	15-16	17-18
'Bidi' smoking	2	5	3
Tobacco 'gutka'	67	21	5
Alcohol-Beer	-	4	10
-Liquor	-	-	2
Total girls questioned	1 33	47	21

It seems the environment is conducive to a large number of girls taking to tobacco chewing (popularly in the form of 'gutka'). This percentage of girls chewing 'gutka' is quite high amongst the girls of the 10-14-age category. About one-third of the girls surveyed in the 17-18 age bracket consumed liquor in some form.

Table 17: **Respondents' preferences for occupations**

Age group	10-14	15-16	17-18
A	20	10	-
B	3	1	-
C	-	2	-
D	1	3	2
E	37	9	5
F	5	4	1
G	39	18	13
TOTAL	133	47	21

KEY: A -Wants to go to school again; B -Wants to work as farm labourers; C -Wants to work as domestic maid; D -Wants to learn weaving; E -Wants to leave the profession (no matter what the future occupation is); F -Wants to learn some kind of skilled labour like tailoring etc.; G -No response

What is obvious from this table is that a fairly large number of girls do not want to continue in this profession - about 25.5%. Most of such girls were below 14.This keenness of under 14 girls to come out of the profession is attributable to the plight of the elderly women around them who in the evening of their life are forlorn and have been neglected by their own kith and kin due to their "expired" commercial value. The young girls apprehend the same bleak future for themselves which explains their detest for the profession. Most wanted training in skills like stitching, tailoring, weaving and so on.

Significantly, not many wanted to work as domestic helpers or as farm labourers. It seems that greater awareness and the fate of the old women folk in their community could contribute to creating a greater desire to leave the profession.

Table 18: **Opinion on the necessity of prevention of commercial sexual exploitation of girl children**

Response	No. Of Respondents	Percentage
Yes	105	52.5
No	49	24.5
No Response	56	28
TOTAL	200	100%

A high percentage of 52.5% indicated the definite need to prevent the sexual commercial exploitation of girl children, while 28% abstained from giving any response.

Table 19: **Awareness of AIDS**

Response	No. Of Respondents	Percentage
Yes	67	33.5
No	133	66.5
TOTAL	200	100%

There is clearly a great deal of ignorance with regard to AIDS/HIV and other STDs. Only 33.5% have only heard about it but they do not know what exactly it means. The low awareness regarding the deadly disease calls for large-scale educational programmes in the transport corridor where prostitution is rampant mainly among truck drivers.

On enquiring about health problems, a majority of the girls belonging to the 14-year category complained of abdominal pain, pain in the neck, joints and shoulder. Occasional body ache was common in women of all age groups. Almost all the above mentioned could be said to be occupationally - induced problems. Some of their ailments may not be work related but it is worth inquiring as to how even the common fever affecting a prostitute is treated by a general practitioner without consideration of the patient's background.

Table 20 **Respondents opinion on whether a good looking girl in the family is groomed by a `role model' within the family to pursue the `parivarik dhanda' (family occupation)**

Age group	10-14	15-16	17-18
Agree	20	23	18
Disagree	5	3	1
Don't know	108	21	3
TOTAL	133	47	21

This was a very sensitive question, the response to which was again given very reluctantly. About 30.5% admitted that this was indeed the case and the responses of the 17-18-age category overwhelmingly affirmed this. It is however equally significant that 66% of the girls avoided the question altogether.

III Lessons learned

Among the factors contributing to the growth of child prostitution are life and living patterns of certain communities in Rajasthan. While no recorded history is available on history of prostitution in Rajasthan, literature connected with princely states suggests that the weakness for women among most of the kings and princes resulted in the presence of a large number of women who entertained the kings and other influential people. This practice later on grew in the form of prostitution among certain community.

The phenomenon of prostitution today is prevalent among TEGs like Banjaras, Rajnats, Kanjars, Bedia and Dehredar etc. A variety of sources indicate that during the medieval period and till the down fall of Mughal empire major concentration of `flesh trade' was in Jaipur area which today forms part of `pink triangle' of sex trade. Traditionally Jaipur and Ajmer have been focus areas of prostitution in Rajasthan. The feed back from the field, discussion with the people and scrutiny of available data and material indicate that there are about 15,000 prostitutes among TEGs and that significant proportions of them are girl child prostitutes. While at the all India level the estimates of girl child prostitutes are 30 per cent of all women in prostitution, the percentage in Rajasthan is very high between 45 to 55 per cent. One reason for this is that the practice of prostitution is family centered - women in the family adopting prostitution as profession and male members of the family (including father and brothers) acting as pimps or procurers. All field information indicates that the entry age into the profession has lowered to near puberty age and in some cases just before that.

The problem of child prostitution is serious among 15 districts of Rajasthan which can be divided into two geographical areas: one comprising of Jaipur, Aware, Ajmer and another consisting of Udaipur- Jodhpur. The seven districts in which the phenomenon of prostituted children is rising at alarming speed are Alwar, Bharatpur, Dholpur, Jaipur, Tonk, Ajmer and Udaipur. Other eight districts: Baran, Bundi, Banswada, Dousa, Dungurpur, Jodhpur, Sawai Madhopur, Sirohi will witness the phenomenon during coming years. Further analyses indicate that singing and dancing girls are mainly located in Alwar, Bhartpur, Dholpur and Jaipur. Concubines are predominantly found in Udaipur and Dungurpur and new phenomenon of call girls is four districts - Jaipur, Ajmer, Udaipur and Jodhpur that have emerged as tourist centre in recent years.

Numbers of reasons have contributed in the growth of prostituted girl children in Rajasthan. In our assessment and feed back increased road traffic between Gujarat and north India due to Kandhla free port and petro - chemical industries located in Gujarat), increased tourism, misconception about STDs and AIDs and no alternative income avenues for men particularly young male members among the traditional entertainer groups are major contributing factors for the growth of child prostitution in Rajasthan.

Major clients are transport operators (drivers and cleaners), migrant labourers, young students and tourist. Surprisingly the percentage of young students among clients may be about 20 per cent in ` pink triangle area'. The business is not confined locally and large numbers of tender age girls are taken to Bombay where they stay for short time and come back. They do not go to `red light' area but to private hotels and houses. Some girls are reported to have visited even the Gulf countries.

The economics of child prostitution in Rajasthan gives us clue to the profits from `selling the fruits of womb'. At the time of deflowering ceremony known as ` nathani utarana' the parents receive about 20,000 to 25,000 thousand rupees. A girl in pink triangle area brings income of Rs 200 - 300 per day to home. The girls who are taken to Bombay return with as much as rupees fifty thousand. During our field study we were informed that the girls returning from the Gulf countries bring home about Rs.150, 000\-. But these are rare cases.

Summarizing the situation, the conclusions are that in case of TEGs nowadays the traditions are used in an instrumental way. The entertainment element has evaporated in the heat of market economy and has been replaced by a set of more exploitative relations in the past. The acceptance of prostitution as an only source of livelihood in the name of tradition can be considered as the survival strategy of the TEGs. Therefore there is no indication among menfolk to change the situation. The women particularly the girl below age of 16 are aware of their situation, that there are limited alternatives for them; that their menfolk are not engaged in other work and thus raising family income, their soco - economic and political situation is so weak that they cannot afford to lose their last strong hold. Majorities of menfolk in TEGs now do very little work other than pimping. The young boys start working as a pimp by the time they are 15 years for their own family members. Some did try to do some coolie work or manual labour job but soon their background haunts them and they are laughed at. Unable to bear this they come back to their `fold'.

Our studies show that they do not work as artisans or craftsmen but they are good at musical instruments and music. In the absence of `multiple survival strategy' failing to provide sustenance the burden of finance falls on women and girls. Strategists, wishing to tackle the problem of child prostitution among TEGs need to seriously explore and do research on how can men among the TEGs could be initiated in acquiring new skills and knowledge so that they get employment in the market. Thus feedback from our study suggests that family household earning is one of the important factors in determining the supply of younger girls by the TEGs. The theory of child labour is at its best here: exploiting their own daughters in horrendous manner. Our study indicates that child prostitution has increased in Rajasthan during past 15 years and that the entry age is lowering down. The girl trafficking has increased in settlements on the highways in the ` Pink Triangle' belt. Besides the fact of its proximity to important centers of growth in Rajasthan there are other reasons that explain the existence of this deplorable trade in human flesh. The reasons of the root causes of, and factors contributing to the growth of child prostitution can be classified as social, economical and the `cultural beliefs and practices'. The situation prevalent among the TEGs could be termed as `civilisational violence' against women (Nagraj, 1997). The onslaught of modernity has not automatically provided protection for the human rights of girl child. Based on the information gathered and data analyzed following conclusions are arrived at:

Economic Factors

In the post independence period, agrarian reforms in Rajasthan have revolved around producer interests and little was done about land reforms after the abolition of Zamindari. The class interests of agricultural workers except in few pocket areas were never strong in Rajasthan. Increasing population pressure and diminishing job opportunities provide excellent ground for exploitation. Some estimates put the average consumption of the poor at below 20 -25 % of the required minimum calorie intake and 50 per cent of children below the age of five years suffer from severe to moderate malnutrition in Rajasthan.

Extreme impoverishment among the TEGs is the most important reason behind the recent phenomenal growth of child prostitution and trafficking. The immediate cause of this practice among TEG's is therefore poverty. Moreover, these communities are discouraged or not allowed to purchase any arable land. As a result, they have not been able to settle themselves down in a meaningful profession, despite the desire and (in rare cases) even the financial capacity to do so. And they do not have the option of a non agro- based occupation because they do not have access to skill training.

Servitude of 'Conscience'

In the face of such limiting options the question of survival dictates that girl children are sold without pro consternation. There are numerous cases of fathers selling their daughters, brothers selling their sisters and husbands selling their wives. Many of these girls are aware what they are being sold for, but they give in. This is servitude of `conscience' due to long suppression.

Social factors

The high concentration of power and privileges derived from the combined effects of inequalities based on class, caste and gender has made for an environment that is extremely hostile to social change and provides ground for oppression of women. One particular symptom of this problem is the brutal repression of social and political movements geared to the emancipation of disadvantaged (Aruna Roy's Right to Information in Ajmer and Srilata Swaminathan's, efforts to organise peasants in Banswara, Rajasthan). Attempts by women to change the situation have been met with violence and rape. (Bhanvari Devi case).

In Rajasthan's caste-ridden society, the TEGs are considered to be of very low status. There is ample information and statistics available which confirm the low status of women and girls in Rajasthan and which depict gender disparities in health, in education and in the labour force. The infant mortality rate in the age group 0-4 years of age for female child is very high in comparison to boys. There is similar pattern of discrimination in education. Net enrolment in the first standard of primary school among the scheduled caste girls is still much lower than other girls. The low status of women is so much entrenched in their psyche that often they reinforce the same selective values by interpreting the male dominated system as the natural order of things and imposing the same social restrictions and ambitions on their daughters.

If this is the condition of women in dominant caste, then one can only imagine the plight of women from the TEGs who are placed at the lowest rung of the social strata. The girls in TEGs have fewer options open to them in terms of education and basic resources in comparison to the girls from other communities. The socialisation process of girls from TEGs is also very restricted. They are not allowed to mix with other girls. Even in schools (if they get to one) they are discriminated. The girls are born to be commodities, destined to be economically dependent, and socially subjugated to their fathers and brothers and later, husband and son. The helplessness that results makes for a resignation amongst the women, which further contributes to the problem.

Highly Lucrative Business

Compared to the low local wage level for a day labourers who hardly earns Rs 20 in the villages, the option of earning 150-200 rupees a day by having one woman in the family solicit clients is a far more attractive alternative. The only other option is migration to the towns where a lot of construction work is going on. With multinational companies like Ericsson, Hansen, Carlsberg moving in, there is a demand for more labourers and better transport facilities. Most often the demand for labourers does not alleviate the villagers plight because town people are preferred to the rustic villagers. So this only means that those already in the flesh trade profit more because of the increase in customers due to increased industrial activities and those employed there. Besides this, the presence of the Bharatpur sanctuary, the tiger den in Alwar and tourist attractions in Jaipur; there is a huge population of travellers in the area. The tourism promotion policies have inadvertently contributed to the growth of child prostitution in Rajasthan.

On an average, the women earn about Rs 75/- to 150/-per day. The price for young girls is higher. When young girls are sold temporarily by families (to learn disco dancing) the families of the girls can be paid anything between 5,000/- and 20,000/-. It is precisely because this is such a lucrative business for the men of the community that the hateful trade continues.

Thus the sex market offers a quantum leap in resources available. It also allows a movement upward in terms of economic aspirations for both consumers and the capital goods that generally require a fairly well to do urban market. All of a sudden these are within the reach of isolated villages. There is an increased potential for change in consumption habits and with them an increasingly penetrating good food and liquor industry. Also one cannot forget the linkages between corruption and sex market.

Development Programmes

The traditional work of agriculture has decreased considerably because irrigation facilities have receded in the last 20 years. A large share of the water is now being utilized by industries. Such a heavy stress on industrialization has made the lives of marginalised communities more insecure. The women and girl children are paying the price for this kind of lopsided development.

There are no openings for employment in agro-based industries or small-scale industries for women in rural areas. If there were such opportunities available many women would take up employment and earn an income to support their families. Where the Bediya and the Raj Nats communities reside even the commonly seen tailoring training centers or weaving and knitting training centers are absent. Families without any substantial earning member, who previously earned a living by entertaining people, have today taken to forcing their daughters into prostitution. The fact that young girls are being thrown to the wolves is proof of the fact that there isn't even the minimum social security that one expects.

There are many programmes for alleviation of poverty like Jawahar Rozgar Yojna (JRY) and Integrated Rural Development Programme (IRDP) but these groups have no access to it. This is equally true of programmes for educating the backward communities. Though the effects of DPEP which seeks to ensure enrolment of all girl children into school, to retain them till the age of 14 years, to improve the quality of education and to improve the infrastructure facilities in education, should have been visible in these areas there is no indication of their work here. Despite the fact that many of the schemes are particularly focused at improving the education opportunities of the backward classes, these schemes like 'shiksha karmi' and 'lok junbish' simply do not reach these communities which traditionally practise prostitution. And most importantly there are development programmes especially for women like DWRCA, 'aanganvaris,' and 'sathin', which the women of the community have not even heard of. So the problem is not that there is a dearth of development programmes and resources allocated for it. The problem is that these efforts simply do not help or reach these communities.

Lack of Rehabilitation Schemes for Children

A very high percentage of women in prostitution want their children, both boys and girls to be taken away and given long term care. They wish there were some kind of a residential school system away from the villages where a different lifestyle can be adopted and different kinds of role models can be looked upped. "Yahan rahenge to yahi karna padega" means that if the children stay with the mothers there is no alternate occupation open to them.

A package Programme needs to be designed to cater to the specific predicament of children of women in prostitution. An extremely important component of this must be to make education available to these children. Despite the fact that there are some schemes that are intended to enhance the literacy rates of the region, since they were not designed with the special sensitivity this class of children require, the programmes do not even reach these children. Rehabilitation schemes have to be sensitive to the particularities of each situation even while being applicable at a macro-level.

Lack of Political Will and Tardy Law Implementation

There have been very limited efforts to solve the problems of nomadic and semi-nomadic communities in Rajasthan. In the late sixties first effort was made by Jawaharlal Nehru, the then Prime Minister of India. Later on Mohanlala Sukhadia made some efforts. After that the issue went into limbus. It is high time that political parties add this to their agenda.

Impact of Consumerism

During the last few years there has been a rapid change in moral values and thinking in our society. The easy availability of blue films, exposure to sex, erotic music and its visuals have adversely affected the minds of young girls and boys especially in these communities where they are constantly exposed to such films and think that "everybody does it" so it must be the norm.

Cultural Factors: In case of the TEGs the most dominant factors that work in enslaving their women in prostitution are culture based. Among the many TEG communities the family structure supports and is organized around sex work. This is seen in the elaborate celebrations surrounding the birth of a girl and again at initiation ceremony into the trade. The TEGs believe that the recruitment of children for expansion of the market is legitimate. Sr. Rozario in her brilliant study also subscribes to this view when she points out that it is not poverty alone which is the cause of prostitution but that poverty " coupled with the existing socio-religious status of women and the prevailing caste structure" are at the root of the evil.

Another prevailing myth among the menfolk is and it is strong in the Rajasthan - that a man infected with STDs can be cured of his ailments by having sex with a virgin. Virgins are usually children.

Today it is AIDS and earlier it was STDs. In addition to this during our study we found that there are lot of cheap porno books which are sold on the footpath in urban areas. They invariably have references to curing by penetrative sex with virgin girls' .The youth, the truck drivers; the half-literate migrant labour class gets highly influenced by these books.

Concluding remarks:

First thing first. We must state that Rajasthan is one of the regions in India that has a high incidence of violence against women and has large presence of nomadic and semi nomadic population and of the groups that we have referred to in our study as the TEGs. It lags behind in many development indicators. And given the overwhelming influence of these indicators, the State has not demonstrated any special concern in development planning towards eliminating commercial sexual exploitation of children. Another astonishing factor noted in our study is `culture of silence' among the people about this situation. Public opinion and actions are important in bringing about any change. Child prostitution is not an issue of the department of social welfare alone. Unless it is projected as an issue of the society as a whole, our study points that we may not be able to cut much ice. In Rajasthan it is prevalent view among academics and public leaders that only Government has ` to do something.' In the field of legal enforcement, yes. But it is the society at large which can effectively put an end to this practice of child prostitution.

It is likely that the emotional responses from those w ho wish to ameliorate the plight of prostituted children will find it hard to agree but it is a fact that current level of available social and economic opportunity for women and men suggests that it is very difficult for them to improve the situation of their children. A more fundamental way of improving the conditions of women TEGs would be to create long term employment with a guaranteed access to this work. And in the short term provide definite plan of rehabilitation as suggested by the women in TEGs themselves. But until alternative is created for them, it will remain story of, " disintegrated and scattered they have bondage their lives only to disrespect, slavery and early death," The need is to move from `protest' to `propuesta': the input and participation of these very social groups in solving the problem. And that is the human rights challenge of the 21st century.

Notes and References

1. Banerji, Sumanta(1994), `Obstacles to Change', Economic and Political Weekly,26 March
2. Basu, Alka Malwade (1992), Culture, the Status of Women and Demographic Behaviour (Oxford: Clarendon Press)
3. Chanana, karuna (1990),"Structures and Ideologies: Socialisation and Education of the Girl Child in South Asia', Indian Journal of Social Science, 3(1)
4. Chanana, karuna (ed.)(1988), Socialisation, Education and Women: Explorations in Gender Identity (New Dlehi: Orient Longman)
5. Dreze, Jean and Amratya Sen (ed.)(1995) India: Economic Development and Social Opportunity (Oxford University Press)
6. Dereze, Jean. & Amratya Sen, (Eds), (1998) Indian Developenmt, Oxford India paperbacks, Delhi
7. Devasia, Leelamma, (1995) Girl Child in India, Ashish Publishing House, New Delhi
8. Dutta, Bhaskar (1994) Welfare Economics, Oxford University Press, Delhi
9. Ghosh, A., U.R.Ananathamurthy, A.Beteille, S.M.Kansal, V.Mazumdar and A.Vanik (1994), Evaluation of Literacy Campaigns in India, report of an independent Expert Group appointed by the Ministry of Human Resource Development (New Delhi: Ministry of Human Resource Development, Government of India)
10.Government of India (1992), Health Information of India: 1991
-----------------------------(1994), Health Information of India: 1991
11. Census of India 1991.
12.Karve, Ishwari (1965), and Kinship organisation in India (Bombay: Asia Publishing House).
13.Kishwear, Madhu (1995), 'When Daughters are unwanted', Manushi
14.Kumar Krishna, 1994,Democracy and Education India (London, Sangam Books)
15.International Labour Organisation, (1997) Child Labour Targeting the Intolerble, Geneva

16.Shanta Sinha, (1995)`Child Labour and Education Policy in India', Lal Bahadur Shastri Academy of Administration, Mussorie,

17.Srinivas, M.N., (1966), Social Change in Modern India (Berkeley and Los Angels University of California Press).

18.UNICEF, (1996) Better Schools : less Child Work, ICDC, Florence, Italy

19.Weiner, Myron (1991) The Child and the State in India: Child labour and Education Policy in Comparative Perspective (Princeton: Princeton University Press).

20.Slaughter. R. A., 1996, New thinking for a New Millennium, Routeledge, London

21.Nalini Rajan, 1998, Secularism, Democracy, Justice, Implications of Rawlsian Principles in India, Sage, Delhi

22.Sudhanshu Mishra, 1998, Rajasthan through Ages,The Observer, Delhi

23.Pal R M , 1995, PUCL Bulletin, New Delhi.

Chapter 6

Vision & Policy Implications

> We must place dignity and development of the individual at the centre of our concern...We owe it to future generations go give a more hopeful start to the 21st century than that which our predecessor inherited nearly one hundred years ago."[1]

Perhaps there is no comparable period in this century that has so dramatically changed the course of human destiny. The Indian sub-continent is characterised by extraordinary geographical, political and socio economic diversity. Despite diversity and complexity the South Asian region has the largest population in the world that is committed to periodic elections, representative institutions, fundamental rights and democratic freedom. It is therefore a region of considerable importance. Until recently it was `believed' in certain circles that one cannot create the benefits of growth without violating at least temporarily the human rights of a substantial number of citizens. But this scenario has changed in the last decade.[2] It is now widely advocated that human rights are integral to development.

In the Indian sub-continent cultural and religious traditions play predominant role. Very little efforts have been made to imaginatively build such concept to articulate principles of governance and democratic accountability that drew on the language and ideas of local traditions but at the same time discarding the `harmful' traditions.[3]

In India the problem of child prostitution is more complicated than in other third world countries where it is directly related to sex tourism. In India commercial sexual exploitation of children has its roots in traditional practices, beliefs and gender discrimination. There are a number of prevalent myths that govern and influence behaviors towards the girl child in India.[4] It is therefore important to create different set of knowledge base in the society. If most optimum results were to be achieved, concerted attack on the problem at the right place and time through a careful planning would be needed. The strategy may also envisage demolishing the barriers created by certain social myths, which block all rational thinking and do not allow a person to see beyond his nose.[5] Our main interest was to collect information, understand the micro level situation, draw lessons and suggested policy formulations for the Indian sub-continent where cultural beliefs play very important role in commercial sexual exploitation of children.

Nevertheless, while carrying out our research we found that very little is known about how certain cultural beliefs are contributing to the growth of child prostitution. Therefore revealing the nature of the problem itself becomes a formidable task.

The data and analysis generated by the case studies have enabled identification of general objectives of intervention in the area of child prostitution. The eradication of child prostitution - paid or unpaid, within the family or outside- will require both long and short-term policies. During the study we found that while poverty alone is not the sole factor responsible for child prostitution, yet the feedback indicates that poverty reduction programmes should be an integral part of the strategy. Without such efforts, more immediate and direct policies addressing the problems of prostituted children will be short lived. Intrinsic to such policies is the need to formulate a more humane and equitable model of development.

Changing attitude towards child prostitution - another essential front on which we have to fight the battle - involves promoting a culture of childhood as enumerated by the Convention of the Rights of the Child and enshrined in the Constitution of India. The fostering of attitudes which recognises the importance of childhood; the importance of education and the importance of healthy education will go a long way towards eradicating the evil of the sex trade. The media can play vital role in creating awareness about 'childhood' and its importance in a person's life.[6] The electronic media, both, government controlled and privately owned, which have a large and more effective reach should take it as a social responsibility.

While long term policies do have their own importance, the short-term measures are equally important. Rescuing children and rehabilitating them should be the prime concern of the government. While planning rehabilitation, structural changes in the education system would be necessary. Elimination of child prostitution can be achieved through effective social control (teachers, parents, and grass root organisations, religious groups, employers, community leaders) as well as through stricter enforcement of legal provisions. Notwithstanding criticism that enacting laws are not enough the necessity and importance of legal deterrent cannot be denied for they serve as a light house for social activists and various agencies of the government.

During our study we found that the phenomenon is worldwide. In USA the average age of entry into prostitution is 14. Up to 90 per cent of prostitutes are under the control of pimps. Seventy per cent of prostitutes have experiences of multiple rapes by pimps and strangers. Prostitution is a 14.5 billion dollar a year business in the United States.

In India, it is estimated to be a Rs 300 crore industry and the number of children suffering commercial sexual abuse in India are between 300,000 to 500,000.[7] The average age of girls forced into the trade has decreased from 14-16 to 10 -14 years. The prostituted children are not confined to big cities alone but are found in rural areas also. The demand for young girls is not new but now the age of the débutantes in the sex dens is decreasing to pre-puberty stage.

These symptoms are indicators of not only moral decay but also of the failures and biases of public policy in the field of education, social assistance and the lack of political will. We fear that greater social cost may have to be paid over the next few years and that the `worst is yet to come' as suggested by information gathered during our study. The approach we propose would require setting up of an `early warning' child monitoring system which would also include data on health status and rates of enrolment of children and a few other indicators. The monitoring system aims at producing a simple `social monitoring report' to be submitted periodically to the government and public opinion.

The feed back during out study suggests that a piece meal project approach to the problem may not make much change and therefore a definite policy framework needs to be evolved.

Policy formulations are a difficult task and that is the reasons while several governments are happy to announce projects and funds available to it but they shun declaring any policy.[8] what are the different policy approaches in general today and what is the importance of various approaches. There are three different models of social policy existing in three different economies- the United States, Germany and Sweden. While discussing the efficiency, cost and underlying philosophy of such three difference models, one message is clear that there is no single model. And the adoption of one instead of another would lead to very different outcomes. Whatever the model may be the targeting of benefits to the needy may help save our scarce public resources. But the limitation of all three models is clear to us. The private insurance model of USA, the social insurance model of Germany and a social assistance model of Sweden will bring its own investment and policy intervention to solve the social problems.[9] With these pros and cons in mind, it is evident that simple cost effective accounting will not suffice in deciding on the relative merits of one or another model. The choice between social policy alternatives depends in the final analysis on the conditions in each country: the composition of its labour force, its demographic profile, its level of economic development and its culture and its political will. This also brings us to the question of different systems: Need-oriented systems, pragmatically evolving systems' and ideologically constructed systems. It is no coincidence that along with the news of child prostitution growing in erstwhile Soviet Union in 1991, India also witnessed the phenomena. In the ideologically constructed systems the historical experience shows that policies are not genuinely geared to satisfy needs but to have a formal proof of the fulfillment of the ideological tenets. While this explanation would be too simplistic to condemn in a wholesale way everything which happened during the past decades in India, the fact remains that the central model of imposing power on reality which were artificially invented, which had no grass roots, which were forced upon society from the top and which, therefore, were never made legitimate by the popular will, did not yield the desired social change.

While designing long term or short term policies, one question which is likely to haunt the policy makers is the question of what should be the attitude towards the parents who deny development rights to their children. The Child's Rights Convention does not recognise the validity of parental exploitation of a child's labour on the basis of economic need. As a human rights treaty, it has imposed duties on states rather than on individuals. By contrast governments in the sub-continent have adopted in general a permissive approach to parental exploitation of a child's labour. Sexual exploitation of children by parents can also be perceived as a form of child labour when it results in the exploitation of children for profit.[10] Research has drawn attention to the legitimacy accorded to child prostitution and trafficking in India through the Devadasi custom of dedicating poor girl children form low castes to goddess or parental power to give very young girls in marriage to older men. These studies indicate how these practices continue with parental and family support despite the existence of regulatory control against the Devadasi practice and child marriage. The Immoral Traffic Prevention Act 1956 was extensively amended in 1986 and contains regulatory controls on prostitution and trafficking that were drafted in the context of the problems that have emerged. A reassessment of the whole approach to parental exploitation of children in prostitution, child labour and marriage is required in order to meet the standards now set by the Convention on exploitation of children and child abuse in family setting. The exploitation of children in all these areas with knowledge and complicity of parents is a problem that has to be addressed in India in a comprehensive manner, combining legislative sanctions with social and economic interventions.

So here are three areas that require public policy attention: the child and family policies, social safety networks and poverty alleviation programmes. Thus a combination of short and long term strategies are required to make dent on the problems.

In the first category of intervention and policy consideration would be direct relief and rehabilitation to prostituted children. The socio-economic condition of the families is such that unless long- term plans of education and alternative skill training is undertaken there is little likelihood of the growth of prostitution and child trafficking being curbed. Here are some suggestions regarding the contents of a package programme:

a) A special single window cell needs to be created and installed in the districts afflicted by this problem. To cut short the bureaucratic procedures, the representatives of Labour, Health, Human Resource Development and Education Ministries along with NGOs and UNICEF representatives should be available to help design programmes that specially cater to the needs of the women and children of the communities which practice prostitution in the name of tradition. The persons in this cell should be empowered to also provide immediate help to children and women in dire situations. Thus there should be a set of immediate contingency plans to assist people in need of prompt help.

b) Since a number of women in prostitution have expressed the desire to extricate their children from the exploitative environment of the settlements it is recommended that at least one such residential school be built in districts having problem of child prostitution. While many believe it would be cruel to take away the only possession of the women (their children) it is forgotten that the women often have aspirations for their children and want that they move on to healthy environment and work situations. Providing education and teaching skills in these schools where all the children of TEGs can share a certain sensibility would be conducive to improving their self-worth and encouraging them into productive and creative activity.

c) Under the Balika Programme of the Government of India (initiated by the Gujral Government) the girls from these communities should be encouraged by giving scholarships. Ambitious programmes for improving the education level are announced but for them to be successful it is imperative that they address the particular needs of the most vulnerable sections. Therefore, it is important that the schools they go to are residential.

d) The health situation these communities need special scrutiny. The knowledge about AIDs and other STDs is scant and faulty. In an era threatened by AIDS, if `communities in prostitution' are not the first to be addressed in health policy then there is something wrong with our emphasis. And we have failed to make this an issue because it is very difficult to make people help a community of prostitutes. Even well educated people have misconceptions about the possible contagion of disease, so one can hardly expect the common person to express concern when it is related to the prostitute.

Misconceptions like the ones where the men believe that young girls do not contract the diseases and in fact cure men who have diseases have to be addressed immediately. For this, a special team has to be set up to decide what message it is that needs to be communicated, what would be the most effective media for it and how it should be taken to these communities. This requires research and professional skill.

e) The state governments should carry out a detailed survey of vulnerable groups in the risk prone district (identified for child prostitution) and the time bound Programme be implemented for poverty alleviation for both men and women. The JRY and IRDP must be specially directed to cover the needs of these families. The NABARD success must be judged on the basis of how many families of these communities have been rehabilitated. There is a need to introduce skill development programmes amongst the adolescent girls and young women.

(f) One of the reasons for the lack of food security is that these communities are discouraged from owning any land. As is the case for leper communities in India the TEGs have no access to land which is the best way of marginalising a community, making them part of the dependent population and denying them rights. A provision should be made to provide arable land to each TEG family so that they can settle down to a life of cultivation and food production.

2. Public Awareness: A special public education programme should be designed in the `pink triangle' to sensitise the people in the area on the practice of forcing women and children into prostitution. Different media should be used to expose the girls to the alternatives in activity, employment and lifestyle. The school teachers in the area must be specially trained in dealing with children from these exploited and marginalised communities. The district publicity officer along with NGOs could prepare social awareness package programme. The social awareness programmes on national TV should be encouraged to document the phenomenon and broadcast it, so that there is country-wide awareness which would put pressure on the authorities in every region. We are now living in an era of information technology and it should be possible for us t0 educate the people about this evil practice.

3. Political Commitment: There is a clear indication that the political parties in India have not considered the question of child prostitution in their agenda. Local party workers can play a major role in stopping the commercial sexual exploitation of children. All major political parties have links with at least one major trade union. The trade union leaders can play a crucial role by creating political pressure in this regard.

4. Legal Measures: Laws on family relations have a clear impact on the treatment of girls and women in society. Although legal measures in themselves are not sufficient to control the problem, any legal change does have a demonstrably positive effect. Therefore, there is a need for the strictest enforcement of the laws against prostitution and trafficking. The existing law that relates to child trafficking is very weak in its intention and even weaker in its application. The hiatus previously identified in the law on child labour in general should be used to address child prostitution. Laws should be reviewed to take into account the customary practices and suitable laws related to check child prostitution in traditional communities should be formulated with the most severe penalty imposed on offending parties.

A new law to deal with the emerging challenge of commercial sexual abuse of children by family itself is required in India.

System of early marriage is clearly linked to health and wellbeing of the girl child. Failure to provide resources and facilities for registration of birth and marriages are crucial for enforcing existing laws. The phenomenon of child marriage produces the phenomena of child wives, and divorcees. The child marriage is one of the gender discrimination, which must be located within the framework of child rights and women's rights.

Education policies in India must intrinsically be perceived as a major intervention to check early entry of children into labour market. In India many pronouncements have been made but holistic, affirmative education policies for girls is yet to translate into time and achievable goals. The major goals of girl child decade are yet to reach masses. The issue of employing female teacher in school seems to be the popular concept on the minds of rural people.

In the best interest of the girl child policies that reflect a common age for expressing consent for sexual intercourse, compulsory education and child labour will help to foster development of women rather than hinder and will prevent sexual exploitation. The proof of age is crucial in rape, child abuse and child labour.

As in other South Asian countries, India continues to adopt non-intervention approach to customs. The 'harmful' customs and traditions have to be stopped. Undermining and intervening in these traditional practices through combination of law, policy and advocacy are important. India should launch decade long campaign against harmful customs and traditions to correct the `historical wrongs'.

5. Co-ordination: If past experiences are any guide, micro level programmes or isolated efforts had to be networked to develop a macro understanding and approach of the problem. Hope lies in the number and strength of links that can be forged between ordinary people's efforts and policy formulation. To tackle the problem of child prostitution a co-ordination committee of district officials, political party representatives, UNICEF, National Commission on Women, National Human Rights Commission, representatives from NGOs and research institutions should be set up. Networking of efforts is an important step to check growing menace of child prostitution.

EPILOGUE

Today short term interventions cannot contain the battle for the bodies and mind of child victims of commercial sexual exploitation .To undermine the aggressive power of the sex industry long term policy interventions would be needed which would envisage reducing poverty, ending gender disparities and preventing fragmentation of families. So far there have been no direct interventions into the home, to check violence, sexual abuse and expatiation. Another area, which needs to be explored, is client directed intervention. This is an area of further research. But to sit idle and do nothing will be criminal. Radical short-term strategies must be found because children cannot wait.

Any struggle for change should be undertaken with a sense of humility. And it should be clear that the kind of actions that brings results in the long run, is a long drawn process. Without people's participation nothing, can change. The creation of political will takes an enormous amount of energy input to produce even a tiny output. Times are changing with regard to media and information access. The process of sensitising the public about such issues has to be handled with sensitivity and requires professional skill. Donor agencies willing to support action to curb child prostitution need to support the advocacy and lobbying work, whiie relief and rehabilitation ought to be primarily looked after by the State.

The media had, and still have, an important role in this battle for a better future for children in the 21st century. Let innocent girls not be sacrificed at the altar of so called 'development'. The civil society needs to ponder over this. From a prospestive to stop commercial sexual exploitation of children two things need to be taken care of.First, the issue is woven into the fabric of society and it is open to interventions at different levels.This sets limits to approaches with singular strategy intervention.So a multiprong strategy for intervention at society, economic and legislative action is required. This will largely depend on the 'social empowerment process'.Second, the political economy of social change will determine the pace with which this problem will receive attention.

In the final analysis, the issue is not of finances but of political will. Nobel laureate Amratya Sen rightly pointed out that the role of education and skill makes it all the more essential to pay attention to public policy to expand basic education and to promote skill formation.[11] The role of widespread education has been quite crucial in countries that have successfully grown fast making excellent use of world markets. The point is not that these countries have a much higher base of elementary education now than India currently has, but that they already had radically higher levels of education in the nineteen seventies. But in India there has been an astonishing failure of adequate public action in expanding elementary education. The persistence of endemic illiteracy and educational backwardness in India has many adverse affects. It limits, in general, the freedom and well being of the masses, and has a direct role in the relative deprivation of women in particular. The situation thus calls on responsible governments to create social opportunities that are valuable in themselves and which can also help the process of economic development. This is the lesson India can learn from history.

Notes and References

1.Mary Robinson, President of Ireland (1993) quoted in Human rights in New Consensus pg. 93(Ms. Robinson is now UN High Commissioner for Human Rights)

2.Tiruchelvam, Neelan Dr. January 1993) Studies in Law and Society, paper, Council of Europe.

3.Goonasekhare. Savitri, 1998, Children Law and Justice, UNICEF, New York. Sage, New Delhi pg. 267

4.In Haram's Way UNICEF, Kathmandu

5.Patnakar.Gedam, 1995, Poverty in India, Deep and Deep Publications, New Delhi

6. Gathia, Joseph, 1998, Children's Rights and Media, paper for 23 rd International Congress of International Federation of Journalists, Brazil.

7.Jubilee Campaign material, 1997, circulated by John E. Rode, UNICEF India Representative, New Delhi

8.Coleman, James. S, 1990, Foundations of Social Theory, Cambridge, and Mass: The Belknap Press of Harvard University Press

9.Ferez. F, 1993. Market Economy in Transition, UNICEF, New York

10.Goonasekere.S.1998, Children, Law and Justice: A South Asian Perspective, UNICEF, International Child Development Centre

11.Sen. Amratya, December 27,1997, lecture in New Delhi

Appendices

APPENDIX 1 CASE STUDIES

Poonam

Our arrival at Chowkiwas caused a lot of curiosity and suspicion among the villagers. While some thought we were customers others were confused by the presence of our female colleague.

Chowkiwas is a hamlet of 15-18 households located on the Delhi-Alwar state highway. It is in Alwar district and falls under the jurisdiction of Ramgarh Panchayat Samiti. The houses in the hamlet are made of bricks with thatched, tin or tile roofs. There were a few having concrete roofs also. All the houses had electricity connection but this was not true of water connection for which the villagers had installed a hand pump by pooling in their own money. There was no primary school in this hamlet. The nearest school was in Ramgarh three kilometers away, offering education upto 10th standard. For higher education one has to go 20 kilometer away to Alwar.

It was in this hamlet that we met Poonam. When a conversation was started, she was quite hesitant and apprehensive about our intentions. But when the purpose of our visit was explained she felt more comfortable. Poonam is 14 years old and stays with her mother and eldest sister. Her father passed away a few years ago. He was an illiterate man who used to work as an agricultural laborer. Poonam's four elder brothers are married and have moved away. Her elder sister, also illiterate, is in prostitution and has three children. Poonam is the youngest child in the family. She never went to school because "nobody from the village used to attend school. School is also too far to go to." She spent her `childhood' playing. But once she was 9 or 10 years old she started helping her mother with household chores.

Her first entry into flesh trade was instigated by a friend who "showed her the way to earn money and enjoy life." Her first customer whom she remembers vividly was a college student whom she entertained at her friend's house. Poonam was a little over 12 years then. Since then she has been entertaining a variety of people from students to officers and lorry drivers.

Poonam gets about 4-5 customers a day and charges anywhere between 50/- and 150/- rupees per client. Earning 400/- rupees a day she gives most of it to her mother for buying household provisions and keeps some of it to buy clothes and make-up. She also saves some part of it in a bank at Ramgarh for her future.

When she was asked about this future that she talks about and her plans for them she replied, "We illiterate people never have any plans for life, we lead our lives on a day to day basis." It is obviously money for a rainy day that Poonam is saving, not in order to move out of this trade (which is not really an option) but to have some fiscal support in her old age. Poonam is not interested in married life, which would consist of none of the charm imagined and would inhibit her present independent state.

Poonam's typical day begins at 6:30-7:00 a.m. She gets ready by 8:00 and has something to eat before she is free to start her day of soliciting clients. While waiting for her customers she talks to her friends and watches the passers by. After lunch her wait commences again and could go on late into the night.

Poonam's source of entertainment is her friends, relatives and television. Her knowledge about AIDS is half backed and she has no clue of the extent of danger of the disease she is exposed to in her trade. She generally gets her client to use a condom though, and foregoes a client if she fails to convince him to use one.

Her mother and sister said that if the government gave them some land as part of some rehabilitation scheme they would leave this profession. After all even women are capable of tilling the fields, they said. They are just waiting for some income generating schemes to come to their area so that plight may be alleviated.

The village headman blames the Meos (who is the Panchayat leaders). They look down upon the practice of these communities to the extent that they do not extend any of the development aid that those under the jurisdiction of this Panchayat would be entitled to. They would even evict the Raj Nats if they had their way. However, it is of course for the men of the hamlet, the village elders themselves to assert their authority and retaliate against the sale of their women's sexuality, which they do not do according to Poonam.

Poonam will continue to practise prostitution till she is about 35 -45 years old at the latest. After that she will have no customer to provide her even her meals. Since she does not want to get married she will not even have a husband to take care of her. She survives on the hope that her children will be in a more productive and sustaining occupation. But one wonders whether Poonam's children will have that good fortune. ●

Roshni

Roshni belongs to Nandlalpura, a hamlet of 20 households near Mahla. This hamlet is about 4-5 kilometres off the Jaipur-Ajmer highway. The houses in the hamlet are mainly 'kachcha' or semi 'pakka'. The settlement has electricity connections but the water supply is poor. The Panchayat installed a hand pump.

Roshni is a tall, attractive, young girl of 14. She belongs to the 'Harijan' community of Raj Nats in Rajasthan. This community used to entertain the kings in their courts. Now with the era of kings faded, the women of this community have turned to the only option offered to them. This community is spread over the districts of Jaipur, Alwar, Ajmer, Bharatpur and Kota.

Roshni has a small family of 4 members. Her 20-year-old illiterate brother is an apprentice at a tailor's shop in Mahla. Being an apprentice he is paid only a small stipend, which suffices as pocket money but hardly, pays for household needs. Her mother, a woman of 46 does all the household chores. While the mother was never in the flesh trade business, the mother's sisters are all in it. Roshni lost her father 10 years ago. Since then Rosin's mother tried to bring in some income to the house by working as domestic help, but has been unsuccessful in the endeavour. The fourth member of Roshni's family is her 6-month-old daughter.

Roshni too is illiterate. In fact Roshni's entire family is illiterate. Roshni's grandfather owned quite a bit of agricultural land but it got divided among Roshni's father's eight brothers leaving a meager 2 acres for each. This was not a particularly fertile plot because of which Roshni's family went through some very hard times. The situation got worse when her father died. Roshni could no longer remain inert to the burden of poverty her family was under.

To ameliorate the situation Roshni first took to prostitution when she was 12 years old. Her first customer was a college student from Jaipur. She became one of many in her village to be initiated into the flesh trade. Presently her family depends on Roshni's earnings for survival.

Roshni does not move out of her village for customers. She charges anywhere from 40/- to 150/- rupees from a client depending upon their paying capacity. It is training from the experienced women of the hamlet that taught her how to determine the paying capacity of the client. She also has a few faithful visitors who go to no one but her and she gets about 700/- rupees a month from each of them. We were told that most of her customers are truck drivers. She gives most of her earnings to her mother and keeps the rest for herself to use on grooming herself. She also saves about 100/- for her child's future. It was the consent, even encouragement from her mother and brother that got her into this trade.

Roshni has a scant knowledge of AIDS. She knows that it is a sexually transmitted disease but has no clue of its consequences and because of this ignorance she does not lose a customer who refuses to use a condom. Roshni is now more aware of such things. Her child was the result of an 'accident' and ignorance, but she does not regret not having had an abortion and is happy with her child.

Roshni's typical day begins at 6 a.m. She helps her mother with some of the household work before she gets herself ready for the day. Her wait is usually extended upto 10 a.m. before which customers do not come. She spends this time with her child and talking to friends. She bathes before lunch and is ready to entertain customers again after 2 p.m. Festival times like Diwali and Holi are particularly busy for Roshni. Her source of entertainment is her child, family and friends. They do not have a television or a transistor but occasionally go to Mahla where VCRs are rented out. When asked about her future plans Roshni confidently says, "I don't have a plan for the future because I don't want to be disappointed. People like us are bound to be disappointed if we make plans for the future." On marriage too her apathy and lack of sentiment are apparent. She says, "What is there in marriage? I am getting more now than I would if I married somebody." Her happiness comes from her child and she hopes to have more lately. Her childhood days were spent playing with the village children, none of whom were ever sent to school. This is something Roshni regrets now despite the fact that she has happy memories of playing and frolicking with her friends.

The village elders say that it is a hereditary occupation for them and have no bad feeling regarding it. They themselves have no qualms about surviving on the incomes of their mothers, sisters and daughters. In their words, "one should be proud of continuing an age-old tradition." However the Panchayat members claim that there has been an improvement with regard to the access to education. Many girls are choosing marriage over prostitution. But those in dire need of money do not have the luxury of marriage and are `soiled' before they are of marriageable age. And after this initiation, whether for want of independence or because of the stigma of their trade they seldom get married. ●

Appendix 2

World Congress Against Commercial Sexual Exploitataion of Children

(Stockholm 27-31 August 1996)

Declaration and Agenda for Action

Declaration

1. We, gathered in Stockholm for the World Congress against Commercial Sexual Exploitation of Children, representing the Governments of 122 countries, together with non-governmental organisations, the End Child Prostitution in Asian Tourism (EC PAT) campaign UNICEF and other agencies within the family of the United Nations, and other concerned organisations and individuals worldwide, hereby commit ourselves to a global partnership against the commercial sexual exploitation of children.

The Challenge

2. Every day. more and more children around the world are subjected to sexual exploitation and sexual abuse. Concerted action is needed at the local, national, regional and international levels to bring an end to the phenomena.

3. Every child is entitled to full protection from all forms of sexual exploitation and sexual abuse. This is reaffirmed by the Convention on the Rights of the Child. an international legal instrument of universal significance (of which there are 187 States Parties). States are required to protect the child from sexual exploitation and sexual abuse and promote physical and psychological recovery and social reintegration of the child

victim.

4. According to the Convention on the Rights of the Child, the best interests of the child shall be a primary consideration in all actions concerning children. and their rights are to be enjoyed without discrimination of any kind. In all matters affecting the child. the views of the child should be given due weight, in accordance with the age and maturity of the child.

5. The commercial sexual exploitation of children is a fundamental violation of children's rights. It comprises sexual abuse by the adult and remuneration in cash or kind to the child or a third person or persons. The child is treated as a sexual object and as a commercial object. The commercial sexual exploitation of children constitutes a form of coercion and violence against children, and amounts to forced labour and a contemporary form of slavery.

6. Poverty cannot be used as a justification for the commercial sexual exploitation of children, even though it contributes to an environment which may lead to such exploitation. A range of other complex contributing factors include economic disparities, inequitable socio- economic structures, dysfunctioning families, lack of education, growing consumerism, urban-rural migration, gender discrimination, irresponsible male sexual behaviour, harmful traditional practices, armed conflicts and trafficking of children. All these factors exacerbate the vulnerability of girls and boys to those who would seek to procure them for commercial sexual exploitation.

7. Criminals and criminal networks take part in procuring and channelling vulnerable children toward commercial sexual exploitation and in perpetuating such exploitation. These criminal elements service the demand in the sex market created by customers, mainly men, who seek unlawful sexual gratification with children. Corruption and collusion, absence of and/or inadequate laws, lax law enforcement, and limited sensitisation of law enforcement personnel to the harmful impact on children, are all further factors which lead, directly or indirectly, to the commercial sexual exploitation of children. It may involve the acts of a single

individual, or be organised on a small scale (eg. family and acquaintances) or a large scale (e.g. criminal network).

8. A wide range of individuals and groups at all levels of society contribute to the exploitative practice. This is includes intermediaries, family members, the business sector, service providers, customers, community leaders and government officials, all of whom may contribute to the exploitation through indifference, ignorance of the harmful consequences suffered by children, or the perpetuation of attitudes arid values that view children as economic commodities.

9. The commercial sexual exploitation of children can result in serious, life-long, even life threatening consequences for the physical, psychological. spiritual, moral and social development of children, including the threat of early pregnancy, maternal mortality, injury, retarded development, physical disabilities and sexually transmitted diseases, including HIV / AIDS. Their right to enjoy childhood arid to lead a productive, rewarding and dignified life is seriously compromised.

10. While laws, policies and programmes exist to counter the commercial sexual exploitation of children, greater political will, more effective implementation measures, and adequate allocation of resources are needed to give effect to the spirit and letter of these laws, policies and programmes.

11. The primary task of combatting the commercial sexual exploitation of children rests with the State and families. The civil society also has an essential role to play in preventing and protecting children from commercial sexual exploitation. It is imperative to build a strong partnership between Governments, international organisations arid all sectors of society to counter such exploitation.

The Commitment

12. The World Congress reiterates its commitment to the rights of the child, bearing in mind the Convention on the Rights of the Child, and calls upon all States in cooperation with national and international organisations

and civil society to:

Accord high priority to action against the commercial sexual exploitation of children and allocate adequate resources for this purpose;
Promote stronger cooperation between States and all sectors of society to prevent children from entering the sex trade and to strengthen the role of families in protecting children against commercial sexual exploitation;

Criminalise the commercial sexual exploitation of children, as well as other forms of sexual exploitation of children, and condemn and penalise all those offenders involved, whether local or foreign, while ensuring that the child victims of this practice are not penalised;

Review and Revise, where appropriate, laws, policies, programmes and practices to eliminate the commercial sexual exploitation of children;

Enforce laws, policies and programmes to protect children from commercial sexual exploitation and strengthen communication and cooperation between law enforcement authorities;

Promote adoption, implementation and dissemination of laws, policies, and policies, and programmes supported by relevant regional, national and local mechanisms against the commercial exploitation of children;

Develop and Implement comprehensive gender-sensitive plans and programmes to prevent the commercial sexual exploitation of children, to protect and assist the child victims and to facilitate their recovery and reintegration into society;

Create a climate through education, social mobilisation, and development activities to ensure that parents and others legally responsible for children are able to fulfil their rights, duties and responsibilities to protect children from commercial sexual exploitation;

Mobilise political and other partners, national and international communities, including intergovernmental organisations and non-governmental organisations, to assist countries in eliminating the commercial sexual exploitation of children; and

Enhance the role of popular participation, including that of children, in preventing and eliminating the commercial sexual exploitation of children.

13. The World Congress adopts this Declaration and Agenda for Action to assist in protecting child rights, particularly the implementation of the Convention on the Rights of the Child and other relevant instruments, to put an end to the commercial sexual exploitation of children worldwide.

Agenda for Action against Commercial Sexual Exploitation of Children

1. The Agenda for Action aims to highlight existing international commitments, to identify priorities for action and to assist in the implementation of relevant international instruments (see Annex I). It calls for action from States, all sectors of society, and national, regional, and international organisations, against the commercial sexual exploitation of children.

2. **Coordination and Cooperation:**

i) Local / National Levels

a) urgently strengthen comprehensive, cross-sectoral and integrated strategies and measures, so that by the year 2000 there are national agenda(s) for action and indicators of progress, with set goals and time frame for implementation, targeted to reducing the number of children vulnerable to commercial sexual exploitation and nurturing an environment, attitudes and practices responsive to child rights;

b) urgently develop implementation and monitoring mechanism(s) or focal point(s) at the national and local levels, in cooperation with civil society, so that by the year 2000 there are data bases on children vulnerable to commercial sexual exploitation, and on their exploiters, with relevant research and special attention to disaggregating data by age, gender, ethnicity, indigenous status circumstances influencing commercial sexual exploitation, and respect for confidentiality of the child victims especially in regard to public disclosures,

c) foster close interaction and cooperation between the government and non-government sectors to plan, implement and evaluate measures against the commercial sexual exploitation of children, coupled with campaigns to mobilise families and communities to protect children from commercial sexual exploitation, and with adequate allocation of resources.

ii) Regional / International Levels

d) promote better cooperation between countries and international organisations, including regional organisations, and other catalysts which have a key role in eliminating the commercial sexual exploitation of children, including the Committee on the Rights of the Child, UNICEF, ILO, UNESCO. UNDP, WHO, UNAIDS, UNHCR, IOM, the World Bank/IMF, INTERPOL, UN Crime Prevention and Criminal Justice Division, UNFPA, the World Tourism Organization, the UN High Commissioner for Human Rights, the UN Centre for Human Rights, the UN Commission on Human Rights and its Special Rapporteur on the Sale of Children, and the Working Group on Contemporary Forms of Slavery, each taking guidance from the Agenda for Action in their activities in accordance with their respective mandates;

e) advocate and mobilise support for child rights, and ensure that adeqtiate resources are available to protect children from commercial sexual exploitation; and

f) press for full implementation of the Convention on the Rights of the Child by State Parties, including requirements for reporting to the Committee on the Rights of the Child in accordance with existing deadlines, and encourage follow-up of countries' progress towards full realisation of child rights in the context of other relevant United Nations organs, bodies and mechanisms, including the UN Commission on Human Rights and its

Special Rapporteur on the Sale of Children.

3. Prevention:

a) provide children with access to education as a means of improving their status and make primary education compulsory and available free to all,

b) improve access and provide relevant health services, education, training, recreation and a supportive environment to families and children vulnerable to commercial sexual exploitation, including those who are displaced, homeless, refugees, stateless, unregistered, in detention and/ or in state institutions;

c) maximise education on child rights and incorperate, where appropriate the Convention on the Rights of the Child into formal and non-formal education for all communities families and children;

d) initiate gender-sensitive communication, media and information campaigns to raise awareness and educate government personnel and other members of the public about child rights and the illegality and harmful impact of the commercial sexual exploitation of children and promote responsible sexual attitudes and behaviour in society. in keeping with the child's development. sense of dignity and self-esteem;

e) promote child rights in family education and family' development assistance, including an understanding that both parents are equally responsible for their children, with special intervention to prevent sexual violence against children;

f) identify or establish peer education programmes and monitoring networks to counter the commercial sexual exploitation of children;

g) formulate or strengthen and implement gender-sensitive national social and economic policies and programmes to assist children vulnerable to commercial sexual exploitation, families and communities in resisting acts that lead to the commercial sexual exploitation of children. with special attention to family abuse, harmful traditional practices and their impact on girls, and to promoting the value of children as human beings rather than commodities; and reduce poverty by promoting gainful employment, income generation and other supports;

h) develop or strengthen. implement and publicise relevant laws, policies and programmes to prevent the commercial sexual exploitation of children. bearing in mind the Convention on the Rights of the Child;

i) review laws, policies, programmes and practices which lead to or facilitate the commercial sexual exploitation of children and adopt effective reforms;

j) mobilise the business sector, including the tourism industry, against the use of its networks and establishments for the commercial sexual exploitation of children;

k) encourage media professionals to develop strategies which strengthen the role of the media in providing information of the highest quality, reliability and ethical standards concerning all aspects of commercial sexual exploitation of children; and

l) target those involved with commercial sexual exploitation of children with information, education and outreach campaigns and programmes to promote behavioural changes to counter the practice.

4. Protection:

a) develop or strengthen and implement laws, policies and programmes to protect children and to prohibit the commercial sexual exploitation of children, bearing in mind that the different types of perpetrators and ages and circumstances of victims require differing legal and programmatic responses;

b) develop or strengthen and implement national laws to establish the criminal responsibility of service providers, customers and intermediaries in child prostitution, child trafficking, child pornography, including possession of child pornography, and other unlawful sexual activity;

c) develop or strengthen and implement national laws, policies and programmes that protect child victims of commercial sexual exploitation from being penalised as criminals and ensure that they have full access to child-friendly personnel and support services in all sectors and particularly in the legal, social and health fields;

d) in the case of sex tourism, develop or strengthen and implement laws to criminalise the acts of the nationals of the countries of origin when committed against children in the countries of destination ("extra-territorial criminal laws"); promote extradition and other arrangements to ensure that a person who exploits a child for sexual purposes in another country (the destination country) is prosecuted either in the country of origin or the destination country; strengthen laws and law enforcement, including confiscation and seizure of assets and profits, and other sanctions, against those who commit sexual crimes against children in destination countries; and share relevant data;

e) in the case of trafficking of children, develop and implement national laws. policies and programmes to protect children from being trafficked within or across borders and penalise the traffickers; in cross border situations, treat these children humanely under national immigration laws, and establish readmission agreements to ensure their safe return to their countries of origin accompanied by' supportive services; and share relevant data;

f) identify and strengthen or establish networks between national and international law enforcement authorities, including INTERPOL, and civil society' to monitor against the commercial sexual exploitation of children: set up special units among law enforcement personnel. with adequate resources and child-friendly facilities, to counter the commercial sexual exploitation of children; appoint liaison officers aimed at guaranteeing child rights in police investigations and judicial procedures for the exchange of key information; and train all law enforcement personnel on child development and child rights in particular the Convention on the Rights of the Child, other relevant human rights standards and national legislation;

g) identify and encourage the establishment of national and international networks and coalitions among the civil society to protect children from commercial sexual exploitation; foster action and interaction among communities families, non-governmental organisations, the business sector, including tourist agencies, the World Tourism Organization, employers and trade unions, computer and technology industry, the mass media, professional associations, and service providers to monitor and report cases to the authorities, and to adopt voluntary ethical codes of conduct; and

h) create safe havens for children escaping from commercial sexual exploitation, and protect those who provide assistance to child victims of commercial sexual exploitation from intimidation and harassment.

5. Recovery and Reintegration:

a) adopt a non-punitive approach to child victims of commercial sexual exploitation in keeping with the rights of the child, taking particular care that judicial procedures do not aggravate the trauma already experienced by the child and that the response of the system be coupled with legal aid-assistance, where appropriate, and provision of judicial remedies to the child victims;

b) provide social, medical, psychological counselling and other support to child victims of commercial sexual exploitation, and their families, paying particular attention to those with sexually transmitted diseases, including HIV / AIDS, and with a view to promoting the self-respect, dignity and rights of the child;

c) undertake gender-sensitive training of medical personnel, teachers, social workers, non-governmental organisations and others working to help child victims of commercial sexual exploitation on child development and child rights, bearing in mind the Convention on the Rights of the Child and other relevant human rights standards;

d) take effective action to prevent and remove societal stigmatisation of child victims and their children; facilitate the recovery and reintegration of child victims in communities and families; and where institutionalisation of the child is necessary, ensure that it is for the shortest possible period in accordance with the child's best interests;

e) promote alternative means of livelihood with adequate support services to child victims and their families so as to prevent further commercial sexual exploitation. and

f) adopt not only legal sanctions against the perpetrators of sexual crimes against children. but also socio-medical and psychological measures to create behavioural changes oil the part of the perpetrators.

6. Child Participation:

a) promote the participation of children, including child victims, young people, their families, peers and others who are potential helpers of children so that they are able to express their views and to take action to prevent and protect children from commercial sexual exploitation and to assist child victims to be reintegrated into society; and

b) identify or establish and support networks of children and young people as advocates of child rights. and include children, according to their evolving capacity, in developing and implementing government and other programmes concerning them.

Annex I

The Agenda for Action refers to many international instruments, recommendations and targets which have bearing on children and their families. They include the following:

the 1930 ILO Convention No. 29 concerning Forced or Compulsory Labour
the 1948 Universal Declaration of Human Rights;
the 1949 Convention for the Suppression of the Traffic in Persons and of the Exploitation of the Prostitution of Others;

the 1957 ILO Convention No.105 concerning the Abolition of Forced Labour;

the 1966 International Covenant on Civil and Political Rights;

the 1966 International Covenant on Economic, Social and Cultural Rights;

the 1973 ILO Convention No. 138 concerning Minimum Age for Admission to Employment;

the 1979 Convention on the Elimination of All Forms of Discrimination against Women:

the 1989 Convention on the Rights of the Child;

the 1990 World Declaration on the Survival, Protection and Development of Children and its Plan of Action;

the 1992 Programme of Action of the United Nations Commission on Human Rights for the Prevention of the Sale of Children, Child Prostitution and Child Pornography;

the 1993 Vienna Declaration and Programme of Action of the World Conference on Human Rights;

the 1993 United Nations Declaration on the Elimination of Violence against Women;

the 1994 Cairo Declaration and Programme of Action of the World Conference on Population and Development;

the 1995 Copenhagen Declaration and Plan of Action of the World Summit on Social Development;

the 1995 Beijing Declaration and Platform for Action of the Fourth World Conference on Women;

the 1996 Programme of Action of the United Nations Commission on Human Rights for the Prevention of the Traffic in Persons and the Exploitation of the Prostitution of Others.

The Agenda for Action takes note of the recommendations of the Committee on the Rights of the Child and the Special Rapporteur on the Sale of Children. It acknowledges the initiatives of many international and regional organisations, including INTERPOL, World Tourism Organization (in particular, the 1995 World Tourism Organization Statement on the Prevention of Organised Sex Tourism) and the Council of Europe (in particular, the 1991 Recommendation No. R91 II concerning Sexual Exploitation, Pornography and Prostitution of, and Trafficking in Children and Young Adults). It also recognises the process of evolving a possible Optional Protocol on the sale of children, child prostitution and child pornography. ●

Appendix 3

Prime time for children: media, ethics and reporting of commercial sexual exploitation of children

This paper was prepared as a working document for the World Congress against Commercial Sexual Exploitation of Children by Aidan White and Kate Holman, International Federation of Journalists, for UNICEF

Introduction

Children aren't considered "hot topics" for the media, not unless children figure in a scandalous or heart-rending story or in some shocking data or statistics.

This conclusion by media and child experts in the United States holds as true today as ever. If child abuse and exploitation have figured prominently in the mainstream media in recent years, it has invariably been in the context of horrifying evidence from court proceedings, or better still, the involvement of some well-known (adult) public figure. American researchers have found that although children under 10 made up almost 20% of the US population, they represented only one in every 60 characters on prime time TV. Children's voices are not heard - especially not by the rest of the community. But then the world of television is not like the real world. Its demography reflects its purposes: to produce audiences for advertisers. Looking at it through the prism of age reveals a population curve that, unlike the real world, but much like the curve of consumer spending, bulges in the middle years of life. That makes children and the elderly relatively neglected.

This analysis of the impact of the free-market is one aspect of prevailing currents of control of media and information sources. Another is the tendency of some governments and state authorities to manipulate information, usually through tight state controls of broadcasting media, to meet political imperatives which often do not reflect the considered needs and rights of abused sections of the population.

It is in this context that media coverage of the commercial sexual exploitation of children, like the other aspects of children's lives, takes place. The media industry is either a commercial undertaking which exists to produce profit, never more so than today with the growth in media outlets, achieved through new technology, bringing ruthless competition for limited markets, or it may be subject to political and state controls. In either case, journalists and media workers struggle to maintain a professional centre of gravity. In reality, it is futile for them to ignore the economic and political conditions in which they work.

Yet media are, unarguably, a major influence on cultural development throughout the world; with a responsibility, many believe, particularly in sectors like public broadcasting, to inform and to educate. The challenge facing media professionals, whether they own newspapers or broadcast media or whether they are employed to gather, edit and disseminate information, is to define rules and regulations by which they work and to articulate principles of performance which are transparent and can be tested in a public manner.

But how? The question, as this paper tries to consider, requires serious examination of the way media work, of how existing principles of accountability apply, and how media must be freed from reins of political and economic control which limit professionalism and undermine ethical standards.

The media's role in the evolution of commercial sexual exploitation is complex. On the one hand, they tell the stories of abused and abuser, through news reports, photographs, documentaries, and drama. But on the other, they can themselves become the exploiter, for instance by creating sexually provocative images of children in news or advertising, or, at worst, as the vehicle for child pornography,or sources of information for paedophile networks and sexual tourism.

Furthermore, the way the media portray children has a profound impact on society's attitude to children and childhood, which also affects the way adults behave. Even the images children themselves see, especially of sex and violence, influencetheir expectation of their role in life.

This paper does not seek to provide easy answers to complex and difficult issues nor to ethical dilemmas. But there are standards to be set and guidelines which media can adopt themselves in addressing the need for a public information policy which provides people with extensive, reliable and ethical reportage about the way children are treated in society. Some suggestions are made in this direction throughout this report and in its conclusions.

Finally, although there is much that can be improved in media performance, the conclusions are not only intended to make media more accountable and journalists more responsive to systems of complaint and public scrutiny. It is also a question of encouraging debate within media about the portrayal of children and their exploitation. This is an issue which defines the good health of a just and decent society and is, therefore, a matter of profound professional concern for all who work in media.

1. MEDIA, CHILDREN AND INTERNATIONAL LAW

The international legislative and regulatory framework relevant to the role of media and the commercial sexual exploitation of children is ample, but not specific. These clauses do not constitute an exhaustive list, but offer some important pointers on the role and responsibility of journalists, and the media in general. For example:

The United Nations Convention on the Rights of the Child (1989) enshrines children's right to freedom of expression (Article 13); to protection of privacy andagainst attacks on his/her honour and reputation (Article 16); and also calls on the mass media to disseminate information and material of social and cultural benefit to the child (Article 17). Articles 34 and 36 commit governments to protecting children from all forms of exploitation, including pornography.

The European Convention on the Exercise of Children's Rights (1996) also emphasises children's right to express their own views in decisions affecting them, and calls on national bodies to provide information on children's rights to the media.

The Council of Europe Recommendation 1286 on a European Strategy for Children (1996) introduces the call for a change in the way children are viewed in society. The media should promote children's right to a healthy and balanced development , and all professionals who come into contact with children should have special training on children's rights (Article 8).

The publicising of children's rights is a first step to increase public awareness and promote change in the traditional view of the child, declared the Council of Europe's Parliamentary Assembly. It highlighted the negative effects of the media on children, and wanted to see more controls over new information and communications technologies.

The Council of Europe's Recommendation No.R (91)11, concerning Sexual Exploitation, Pornography and Prostitution of, and trafficking in, Children and Young Adults, is an important one. It highlights the medias role in reporting this issue by inviting them to contribute to a general awareness of the subject and to adopt appropriate rules of conduct. It also warns against the abuse of children's images and voices in an erotic context. On the matter of law, it judges that while the public should be informed about the conviction of child pornographers, the identity of victims and alleged offenders should be protected. And it demands an end to publicity for sex tourism.

The Council of Europe Recommendation No.R (85)11 on the Position of the Victim in the Framework of Criminal Law and Procedure draws attention to the interests of the victim, and the need to protect him/her from any publicity which will unduly affect his (sic) private life or dignity. And **Recommendations No.R (92) 19 and No.R (89) 7** focus, inter alia, on the use of new information technologies for the distribution of pornography.

European Union legislation also refers to the issue in its 1989 **Television without Frontiers** Directive, (Article 22) which bans programmes which might seriously impair the physical, mental or moral development of minors, in particular those that involve pornography or gratuitous violence. Yet it provides a get-out for broadcasters who select broadcast times or use technical measures to ensure that minors would not normally have access to the programmes.

2. RAISING AWARENESS OR SENSATIONALISING: A TWO-EDGED MEDIA KNIFE

The important role which media can play in raising public awareness of the abuse of children and in combatting all forms of criminal and sexual exploitation is well understood. But the issue is not as clear cut as many would like; media coverage can shine the spotlight on those directly responsible, but the victims all too often are also caught in the glare of publicity.

In the report of the Council of Europe's Committee on Crime Problems, the experts emphasised the responsibility of the media and their potential contribution to any policy aimed at preventing the sexual exploitation of children and young adults. The term media denotes here any means of expression transmitting a message for individuals or groups. In its broad sense therefore, the term covers means used for conveying information, such as the printed press, books, radio, television, videograms and advertisements; it also includes the 'producers' who use such media (publishing firms, radio and television companies and advertising agencies etc).

The Committee of experts warned:

Often the mass media function as a two-edged knife in this area of concern. The unravelling of sensational sex and crime cases involving children and young adults tends to overemphasise the issue and to blur the picture. Sometimes, though, it is the media which help to uncover cases of sexual exploitation and to raise awareness of the problem.

But it is also the media that generally infiltrate the public with liberal and tolerant attitudes towards child pornography and prostitution or provide the ways and means (for example advertisements) by which this sex gratification may be achieved. Therefore, their co-operation and their orientation towards safeguarding the rights and the dignity of children and young adults is extremely important.

In February 1996, the **Guardian** newspaper printed a two-page article by the award-winning reporter Maggie O'Kane. It described the life, and death, of girl prostitutes on the streets of Bradford, in England. It was a sensitive, perhaps overly-emotive, yet gripping piece of writing; accompanied by a useful set of proposals for supporting the 'street kids'. Next to it, was a sizeable photograph of an anonymous 13-year-old prostitute, with her shirt open to her waist.

This was the angle which alarmed Eva Aurland, Youth Coordinator of the International Confederation of Free Trade Unions, which has launched a major campaign against child labour. She condemns the picture as sensationalist and unnecessary. Her view is shared by Rachel O'Brien of the Children's Society in the UK, which helped with O'Kane's investigation. Child abuse victims in homes would not be photographed, their identity would be protected, she argues. Yet once on the streets, although they are -- in the law's eyes -- suffering assault every day, they are 'fair game'.

It cannot be denied that the media play a crucial role in bringing the horrors of child exploitation into the public arena, and can be extremely influential. American research reveals that 72% of the public obtained knowledge of child abuse from newspapers, 56% from radio and TV. In 1992, a Swiss journalist arranged a child sex-tour through a travel agent. He wrote such a devastating account of the agent's operation, that the subsequent public outcry forced the agent out of business. At the same time, media coverage of prosecutions under laws against sex tourism, now in operation in at least 12 countries, also helps to warn off men who might be tempted by the idea.

There can be dangers in saturating the public with too much exposure of the issue, thereby creating acceptance and indifference. Many observers have warned of the public's "famine fatigue" when exposed to persistent, harrowing images in television coverage of recent disasters in Africa. The same problem may arise if coverage of children remains singular in its focus on the plight of the victim or the salacious nature of the offences involved.

Media researcher Nancy Signorielli sees two sides to sensationalism: Although child advocates may argue that sensational coverage distorts and exploits a serious problem - perhaps doing more harm than good - sensationalism solves several editorial problems; that is, it can be the response of reporters and editors trying to fulfil the responsibility to cover serious social issues, while continuing to turn a profit. Sensationalism permits an important but unpleasant topic to be covered in such a way that it still captures the readers' attention - and sells magazines.

Eva Aurland would like to see the media place more emphasis on the role of the police, politicians, and other authorities in protecting the children, rather than the children themselves. Her colleague at the ICFTU Elsa Ramos agrees, urging more analysis of the social causes: the pimps, the drug culture, the parents in poverty who are proud to have sold their daughters for a sum which will enable them to support the rest of the family. 'Media should not be so shy about putting the blame on the individuals responsible for the exploitation, and the governments who condone it," she says. For example, newspapers which uncovered the activities of a Bolivian lawyer who, they alleged, paid kidnappers US$40 for a boy whom he sold to a Belgian couple for US$10,000.

But media organisations must invest more time and effort into investigating such stories, if they want to avoid falling foul of defamation laws. It is easier to interview the children, who are hardly likely to sue. In a time of down-sizing and falling editorial expenditure on training and investigative journalism generally, the outlook for more in-depth media coverage is bleak.

Nevertheless, media need to broaden the scope of reportage. The story of child sexual exploitation in general and its commercial aspects in particular is not being told in full. To examine how this can change requires a look at the professional freedoms which journalists require to work effectively, a summary of the principles or guidelines journalists and programme-makers should follow, and the pressures -- legal, financial, or cultural -- which are standing in the way.

3.SETTING STANDARDS FOR MEDIA

The work of journalists, broadcasters, and media organisations is regulated at four different levels:

1. Codes of Conduct: Most journalists usually have their own professional codeof ethics, formulated by trade unions or professional associations. Usually a form of self-regulation;
2. Guidelines: Media organisations themselves, especially in the public service broadcasting sector, may draw up guidelines for professional conduct. Usuallya form of self-regulation;
3. Structures for Regulation: certain regulatory bodies, such as press councils, may be established each with different powers and responsibilities and which may, or may not, have the force of law to support them;
4. Legislation: the law may be used to underpin notions of professional journalism and the systems set out above. The law may also support structures for licensing journalists and regulations providing penalties for breach of ethical conduct.
Legislation circumscribing the media and commercial sexual exploitation of children includes laws for the protection of children, such as the withholding of information identifying children in court cases, in care, or as victims; laws to protect children from moral corruption; laws restricting pornography; and general laws on freedom of expression.

The Canadian Criminal Code, for instance, makes it an offence to publish anything that depicts a child performing a sexual act or assuming a sexually suggestive pose while in a state of undress. In Norwegian law, on the other hand, there is no general protection of public morals, except for a ban on pornographic material.

With regard to codes of professional conduct, we have found no journalists' organisation which offers a specific code of good practice for covering the commercial sexual exploitation of children.

It must be said that although journalists are conscious of a values-related system in which news and information is reported, many of them are ignorant of the form and exact content of the codes of conduct to which they work. There are no clearly established international standards, although the **IFJ's International Code of Principles on the Conduct of Journalism**, agreed in 1954 and now under review, contains the key elements of a journalist's ethical responsibility. Any code will reflect standards of journalism according to understood values within society. It will also deal with questions of enforcement and disclosure, often accepting that openness enhances accountability, credibility and, ultimately, freedom.

Inevitably, the role of codes of ethics in journalism, which begin with sweeping generalities, becomes important when resolving the ethical dilemmas which will arise in particular cases of reporting. In the area of reporting on children and commercial sexual exploitation, there are four closely-allied ethical dilemmas surrounding professional conduct and investigation of the subject:

- o Confidentiality of sources;
- o Undercover journalism and use of subterfuge to obtain
- o information;
- o Co-operating with, and making information available to law
- o enforcement agencies; and intervening in events under
- o observation;
- o Identification of individuals.

a) Confidentiality of Sources

The right to safeguard the anonymity of sources of information is crucial to the journalist's ability to investigate. In Sweden and other Nordic countries, this right is enshrined in law. An Act passed in 1993 in France laid down that:

Any journalist who appears as a witness concerning information gathered by him in the course of his journalistic activity is free not to disclose its source.

The law also controls searches of media premises, which must not obstruct journalists in their work. However, in most countries journalists have to fight to defend this right, often risking fines or imprisonment in the process. The Canadian Broadcasting Corporation in its Journalistic Standards and Practices, for instance, upholds the principle of freedom of information and considers the protection of a journalist's sources to be an important element of this principle, but it reminds journalists that 'protection of sources is not a legal right'. CBC says it will not advise employees to defy a court order, but will provide legal counsel.

Lars Bruun, in his review of ethical codes, found that 42 journalists' organisations around the world made mention of professional secrecy. For instance the Nigerian Union of Journalists' Code of Conduct reads: It is against the ethics of the profession to divulge information received in confidence, no matter what the consequences.

This principle was given backing in law in 1981, when the High Court of Lagos State ruled that the Senate of the National Assembly had exceeded its authority in summoning a journalist to disclose the confidential sources of an article. Often, the court's decision as to whether a journalist may legally withhold the identity of sources depends on the circumstances surrounding the case. In Japan, for instance, the Sapporo District Court interpreted the Code of Civil Procedure as allowing journalists to treat sources as 'an occupational secret', unless the information was required to ensure a fair trial:

A journalist alleged that parents were complaining about child abuse in a local nursery school. The owner of the school sued the journalist for erroneous and defamatory reporting. Under questioning, the journalist refused to identify his sources. The courts upheld his privilege on the ground that, when a fair trial is not at issue, compelling disclosure of confidential sources would improperly impair the reporter's pursuit of his profession.

Journalists recognise that betraying sources not only inhibits their own ability to investigate; it also makes it more difficult for every journalist to work, and may even put their lives at risk, as well as the safety of the informants. The exploitation of children is such a sensitive issue that many abuses would never be revealed unlessthe people who provide the information: children, prostitutes, carers, and many others, could be confident that their anonymity would be preserved. Strengthening the journalist's rights in this area should be an element in any strategy aimed at creating the best professional conditions in which to examine the process of commercial sexual exploitation of children.

b) Undercover Journalism

Ethics codes are useful and they work most of the time. But sometimes genuine conflicts arise between values, and ethical decision-making is required. This difficult skill is like other skills of journalism: it takes training, time and effort to become good at them.

The classic conflict of values comes when a journalist believes it is necessary to abandon the rule of truth-telling, by telling lies or using subterfuge in order to obtain or confirm information, especially about illegal activities. In her review of 28 codes of ethics in 26 European Countries, Tiina Laitila found that 86% made reference to the use of fair means in information collection. However, the definition of 'fair' is open to debate. Clause 5 of the Code of Conduct of the National Union of Journalists (UK and Ireland) states :

A journalist shall obtain information, photographs and illustrations only by straight-forward means. The use of other means can be justified only by over-riding considerations of the public interest.

Deciding when the public interest becomes 'over-riding', and what 'other means' are permissible, is left up to the conscience of the journalist, or often to the employer. This clause affirms that journalists are entitled to exercise a personal conscientious objection to the use of such means.

But the conditions in which "other means" apply need to be carefully monitored. It must be borne in mind that the pressure of commercial competition, and the consequent imperative to be first with sensational news, often contributes to a climate in which subterfuge and 'cheque-book' journalism become standard practice, not for reasons of public interest but primarily for reasons of circulation and commercial advantage.

The challenge facing journalists and those who support high standards of journalism is to create the conditions for sound professional judgement. Sometimes decisions may coincide with commercial advantage; often they will not.

Most ethical guides would acknowledge that it may be ethical to lie, but any journalist who faces such a dilemma must be convinced of the relevance and weight of the public interest, conscious of the harm it might do to credibility, and willing as soon as possible to face a "publicity test" -- public scrutiny of the circumstances.Journalists investigating the commercial sexual exploitation of children should consider carefully whether it is justifiable to lie to, or deceive, either the exploiters, or the victims, in order to uncover the facts.

In her analysis of honesty in investigative journalism, Jennifer Jackson calls for an 'emotional' allegiance to truthfulness: a hatred of lies.

Yet our allegiance to truthfulness needs also to be in part rational; it needs to be reflective, judicious. While it will not normally even occur to people of honest disposition that the end they seek might justify telling a lie, such people can recognise that in quite exceptional circumstances, the end they have in view does justify their lying. They will, of course, reach such a decision reluctantly and with caution...

Journalists can apply the 'publicity test' in advance of an investigation by assessing whether the public would regard the deception as justified. But they should also ask themselves whether there is no alternative route to the story, which does not involve lying.

It is unlikely that the public would object to the subterfuge employed by Dutch programme-maker Aart Zeeman who used a hidden camera in order to track down the makers and vendors of child pornography in Amsterdam. Jackson herself concludes:

It may be suggested that investigative journalists who are prepared to lie to get their stories (and the editors who print their stories) are hypocrites, lying in the name of truth. Yet...lying in order to detect and expose lies is not necessarily hypocritical; sometimes it may be morally necessary or permissible for a journalist to lie, and then the journalist's lie will (when revealed) appear justified even to those who are really honest, who genuinely care about truthfulness.

Nevertheless, an assumption that media are always licensed to deceive in order to get a story, undermines the moral authority of journalistic ethics. In the context of the commercial sexual exploitation of children there are important distinctions to be drawn, particularly because it is not just the pimps and pornographers who are involved, but the children themselves.

A researcher who interviewed children working the streets in British cities, for a Channel 4 documentary **The Care Connection**, remembers: 'For the first 10 or 20 seconds they were very suspicious. But as soon as they realised we were not the police they immediately relaxed. They just opened up completely. They saw that we werenot going to take anything from them - or give anything to them. And once they started talking they wouldn't stop. They came to trust us.'

But there are times when the media do take something from the children. Their exploitation by media professionals in pursuit of a 'good story' or an award-winning documentary can damage, even unintentionally, the dignity and self-esteem of children.

There is an ethical line to be drawn between subterfuge required to uncover the largely illegal activities of exploiters, and investigation of the children themselves. This may not be easy, given that working 'undercover' generally means total secrecy. But the fact that so many of the children are eager to find someone they can trust and who will listen to them, underlines their vulnerability. Experience of deception will further damage their self-esteem, and their relationship with others.

Journalists and media organisations need to apply the highest possible standards of honesty and openness when dealing with exploited children. In practical terms, this means a greater emphasis on ethical questions in journalists' training, to encourage 'a more finely tuned moral sense' . This should focus on concrete examples of specific dilemmas, including the coverage of children's exploitation. It also requires a constructive and supportive debate within newsrooms about these issues, as well as a greater awareness and sensitivity within the media about public attitudes on child pornography and exploitation.

c) Co-operation With The Authorities

Just as journalists are committed to "truth-telling" they are, as citizens, called upon to respect notions of community. Should journalists work hand-in-hand with the authorities and law enforcement officers in reporting on child exploitation? It is a complicated question, on which little guidance is given by formal ethical codes.

Aart Zeeman's team followed the Amsterdam police for a year while making their documentary. However, this can also be a dangerous strategy. In Taiwan, one of the major television stations recently broadcast film of reporters accompanying police on raids of bars and brothels. It included scenes of young men and women being questioned, apparently without any special regard for minors, and with only token efforts to avoid filming their faces. (It is important to recall that there is a newspaper tradition behind most ethics codes and sometimes this does not address the problems of broadcasters. Occasionally journalists involved in "live" coverage may unthinkingly transmit material which causes harm. In such cases, the technology may rob a television producer of the time for reflection which is vital to sound ethical decision-making.)

It is vital that journalists do not become identified in the public mind with security forces, for exactly the same reasons which apply to the protection of sources. But does this mean that journalists who discover evidence of illegal trafficking or exploitation of children, for example, should not pass it on to the authorities?

Again, this is not an unusual dilemma, but it is one of the most difficult to resolve. Convincing arguments can usually be marshalled for and against almost every case. It is a dilemma which depends upon the circumstances, and the conscience of the individual journalist. Aart Zeeman believes the media should not behave as 'the third or fourth arm of the police', and would not want to pass on data outside that broadcast in the programme. His view is that anything which serves to link the media more closely with law enforcers, in the minds of those supplying information will make them more reluctant to talk to journalists in general.

However, other professionals we spoke to did not find the issue so clear cut.The BBC's Chief Advisor on Editorial Policy James Boyle said the Corporation would allow supplementary material to be taken away only if it were clearly in the public interest, and that no danger to any member of staff would result. Brazilian journalist Roberto Mader judged that he would pass on information only to help the girl prostitutes he interviewed in Latin America. In general, media professionals agree that criminal investigation itself is the job of the police and should be clearly separated from the exercise of journalism.

But in countries suffering first-hand from the effects of sex tourism and growing exploitation, it is perhaps natural that journalists' associations and media themselves should feel justified in taking a more proactive role. The Vietnamese Journalists' Association, for instance, states that the media do cooperate with authorities such as police, drug agencies, and families, to prevent the commercial sexual exploitation of children; and that some offenders have been brought to trial as a result.

In Taiwan, in 1990, a child prostitute in the Huahsi Street red light area left a note for passers-by appealing: 'please save me'. The China Times Weekly took up her case, and pressured the Wanhua District police into searching for Lite Chen, as she signed herself. At that time, says Cheryl Lai of the Association of Taiwan Journalists, the authorities paid little attention to child prostitution. But because of the media publicity, the police finally tracked down 14-year-old 'Little Chen', and she was returned to school. This is one case where the police were forced to act by media intervention.

This example raises the question of the role of media in taking up child exploitation cases. Journalists see themselves as neutral observers, but there may be times when the offences they see being committed are so appalling that they must intervene. Again this is a question for individual conscience, bearing in mind all the factors referred to above, but it may be a legitimate role for media to play in certain circumstances. For instance, many journalists reporting the war in Bosnia have witnessed atrocities, but only two of them have agreed to take part as witnesses in the war crimes trials in the Hague: British journalists Martin Bell, and Ed Vulliamy. Bell recognises that he would be a Serbian target if he returned to Bosnia as a reporter. Both journalists accept that 'Many colleagues think that to have given evidence is bad professional ethics.'

However, Vulliamy draws a distinction between 'objectivity' -- a journalist's duty to report the facts -- and 'neutrality' :
At a certain point, the perpetration of atrocity crosses a line, and breaches not only international law but the bases of civilisation.

Beyond this point, he argues, 'neutrality' becomes complicity. The same criteria can very well be applied to child exploitation. The International Federation of Journalists

- although respecting the rights of conscience of individuals -- notes that by taking sides, journalists not only endanger their own safety, they can put their colleagues at risk.

d) Identifying the Victims

If journalists have a duty to the truth in their reporting and to independence in their work they also have a responsibility to minimise harm from their actions, particularly to people who are themselves the victims of injustice and abuse.

The Guardian, which generally adheres to a high standard in its news coverage, is not alone by any means in publishing photographs of child prostitutes, even under arrest. This is particularly true of western media images of children in developing countries, although the technique of obscuring part of the face is now sometimes used. However, more often it is the adult -- the suspected abuser -- whose identity is hidden. In Taiwan, however, there is now a law whereby the names and photographs of convicted pimps and clients of underage prostitutes, and the hotel where the violation occurred, "should be published" after conviction.

Interpol confirms that many countries have legislation protecting the identity of children involved in court proceedings, children in care, or children who are subject to abuse, but laws vary according to who they protect, and under what circumstances. They generally apply to young people under the national age of majority. There is also some controversy about how energetically they are enforced. The Council of Europe's Committee of Experts emphasises this aspect:

The disclosure, during administrative and judicial proceedings, of information which may serve to identify the victim, is a particularly important aspect of secondary victimisation. The psychological consequences of such disclosure may be particularly serious for the children and young adults concerned and are liable to deter the parents or those responsible for the young person from lodging a complaint.
...The dissemination of such information by prosecuting authorities, courts or administrative authorities may cause harm to the young victims of sexual exploitation. The Committee strongly emphasises that cases must be handled with due respect to the victim's privacy.

Despite widespread international understanding of this question, in South East Asia,a newspaper printed the names of two children who had given evidence in the prosecution of a foreign paedophile. Child protection agencies believe legislation should allow offenders to be prosecuted without children being required to testify against them, to avoid any risk of identification or publicity. In Norway, a similar law means women do not have to give evidence in cases of domestic violence. Otherwise, there is a danger of what the BBC calls 'Jigsaw identification':

This happens when different news organisations give different facts associated with the victim which can be pieced together.
It advises staff:
Take care not to give an address, any link with another person in the story, or any link between the victim and the scene of the assault...One way or another,we must not complete the jigsaw.

Victims in general cannot be sure that their identity will not be made public. For instance, the Canadian Broadcasting Corporation guidelines

recognise that:
Broadcasting the identity of a crime victim most often only adds to the person's grief, anguish and trauma.

The CBC tells staff not to broadcast the names of victims, especially of crimes against the person, such as sexual assault. Yet alleged victims of assaults that have not been proved in court are not offered the 'privilege of anonymity'.

Child prostitutes are often afforded even less protection than other young abuse victims, creating an understandable reluctance to report their exploitation. This perception that once children are working on the streets, in bars, taking drugs, or otherwise participating in the world of adult vice, they forfeit the rights of innocent children, is shared in some quarters of the media as well as the law enforcement agencies.

In a survey of five Taiwanese daily newspapers, Chi Hui-jung discovered a general hostility to young prostitutes. Out of 133 news items about arrests for offences involving underage prostitutes, 34.% used unsympathetic headlines, and 35% were unsympathetic in content, using language such as childish; selling herself, deflowered; doesn't study but sells her body; and slut. She concluded that crime reporters do not see the juveniles involved as minors, but use adult standards to judge and blame child prostitutes, and rarely see them as victims. On the other hand, the same reporters are very tolerant towards the clients. Only 4% of the headlines were negative about them, and 91% did not mention them at all, in common with 71% of the reports.

Rachel O'Brien believes such figures reflect a lack of recognition around the world that a crime is being perpetrated by an adult. It should never be the children who are cautioned or condemned.

One interesting conclusion to emerge from the Taiwan study, highlighted by Cheryl Lai, is that ethical standards vary widely between reporters covering different beats:
Most media reports on this issue originate in arrests and thus from the police, and are filed by reporters on crime beats, who are generally less

likely to consider the interests of the children involved, or make serious efforts to protect their identities. Journalists covering disadvantaged groups in society who are generally sympathetic to the movement to abolish child prostitution, take greater care in their reporting not to add to the harm already suffered by the children.

Where children are not specifically protected by law, it is the journalist or editor who must take the decision on whether to identify them. There are some who are even prepared to flout the law for the sake of a sex sensational story. This is particularly damaging in countries with strict contempt of court rules, where the media revelation of unauthorised details in advance of a court hearing can lead to the case collapsing. Even when children themselves are not named, details may be given which endanger them. One newspaper, for instance, which interviewed an 11-year-old boy, boxed out his face in the photograph, but went on to name his sugar-daddy and the streets he worked. He remained at the mercy of a dangerous, violent street culture which has, in the end, as much to do with power and money as sex.

The issue of identity is at the heart of journalistic endeavour. It is in the nature of journalism, from the first lesson in journalism school onwards, to provide facts, including personal details about whoever is involved in a story. The decision to suppress information has to be carefully considered, but the nature of commercial sexual exploitation of children should always encourage a journalist to respect, above all, the rights of the victim. Sometimes, this may not be easy. June Kane, UNICEF's Media Coordinator for the World Congress, calls on documentary makers to think twice before using footage of bar girls in Asia, for example, but will a producer working on a programme about bar girls, be able to alert viewers to the real tragedy of sex tourism, without picturing the girls at work, or telling individual children's stories?

4. MEDIA MYTHS AND STEREOTYPES

In the material provided for the World Congress there is a call to the media to avoid exploiting and victimising the children in their coverage, and to depict them in a way which maintains their dignity. It is a brave, but challenging call. To achieve this, media professionals need to re-examine their old habits. Peter Almond points out that a collection of myths 'contaminate' the public's, and the media's, perception of children.

The media cling to these myths; they are familiar, convenient, easily adapted to conventional formats of news and entertainment. In short, myth is easier to report than the more subtle and complicated reality.

Such myths can lead journalists to mould exploited children into typecast roles as sinners or victims. Families in developing countries, people living in poverty, or victims of war and disaster lose their individuality and their humanity. Victims are portrayed as helpless sufferers, unable to act, think, or speak for themselves. Whole countries and communities become categorised under generalised headlines.

In Thailand, the portrayai of girls from the north of the country drifting into prostitution has become so pervasive that a special project has been launched to protect some of those at risk. Quoted in The Nation, one 13-year-old protests: 'I get angry every time I hear people say that many northern girls are engaged in prostitution. I have not the slightest intention to become a prostitute'.

In 1995, Dr Magda Michielsens of the University of Nijmegen in the Netherlands analysed the portrayal of victims, in the news output of seven TV channels across Europe. She concluded that victims generally are given low status. Victims of violence, disaster, and human rights abuses in developing countries, (she collected examples from Africa), are much less likely to be identified as individuals and offered the chance to speak, than those from Europe. This form of racism reinforces the sense of distance, of 'otherness', experienced by the European or northern viewer.

In a survey of magazine coverage of child abuse in the United States, Nancy Signorielli found that victims were rarely reported to react to their abuse. Women's magazines covered the issue more frequently than news and business magazines, but in a more sensational way. As a result, men were less exposed to the problem. Gerbner also discovered that a high proportion of children on TV appeared as victims.

Disproportionate preoccupation with even sympathetically presented or 'accidental' victims in an under-represented population, relative to exhibiting their own share of numbers and exercise of power, diminishes and degrades that group.

Fierce commercial competition is one factor leading the media to exploit victims, suggests Dr Michielsens. The exposure of emotions and sensationalisation of events attract audiences and sell news. Cash-conscious media organisations apply greater pressure on news teams for productivity. Journalists, therefore, sometimes take the ill-considered, easy route to news-gathering, perpetuating -- whether consciously or unconsciously -- the sorts of myth and stereotype identified by Peter Almond. In this process individuals and groups are not treated with respect and their needs and views are not properly appreciated. Some media organisations are becoming aware of the danger of dehumanising victims in far-away places. James Boyle says the BBC now has clear rules, which apply even to dead bodies. 'Human beings have the same dignity all over the world'. There are a range of approaches being developed, to avoid stereotyping and victimising exploited children, while at the same time telling their story accurately and vividly.

Roberto Mader felt that all the programmes he saw about children's exploitation in Latin America and other southern countries, while strongly denouncing important human rights abuses, left the impression that nothing could be done. 'All you feel at the end of the programme is depressed. Now all my work is about trying to show, not that life in Brazil is wonderful -- we have our problems -- but I work in areas where I know there are people doing very positive things to change the reality in which they live. That is the most important thing: to show how people are getting empowered.'

In search of a 'strong movement' in the Brazilian cities, Mader settled on the Casa de Passegem, a half-way house for girls escaping prostitution. 'It was the only project I found where the girls were having a say about the running of the programme. That was very important. There's one interview where one of the girls says: 'These people used to make me feel so ugly, but now nobody needs to say I am beautiful, because I know I am'.

The girls were shown in a very positive light. Everybody is tired of seeing the negative side'.

Tony Dowmunt, the producer of Casa de Passegem , says all the girls interviewed were over the age of consent, and spoke about their past lives. 'We wanted to show that it was possible to get off the streets'. He believes the media should investigate more of the racist and imperialist dynamics behind sex tourism, which is 'not just a few dirty old men going abroad'.

'In the 1980s, these issues were just starting to be aired. We are still in a backlash, where some of them are considered too difficult to deal with. It is very difficult to find thoughtful discussion about them. '

Roberto Mader believes language is another obstacle to the documentary format. Subtitles are expensive, and often unpopular with audiences. Broadcasting organisations tend to avoid them. 'It's an excuse not to listen to people at all - you just have a voice-over soundbite. Yet people are amazed when they see ordinary people speaking'.

Aart Zeeman traced children back to Hungary, the Czech Republic and the Philippines, but avoided identifying the former victims he interviewed. 'I don't think it adds anything to show their faces, unless they are grown up now and choose to tell their story. Children don't understand the impact being on TV can have. I think you have to be very careful to protect the children -- the film might be shown in the countries where they are living and could easily get them into trouble'.

Altering the names of people and places is one obvious answer for newspaper journalists. But for the documentary maker, the dilemma between using images which will keep the audience's attention, and not endangering or victimising the children, cannot be easily resolved. For The Care Connection, programme makers 'invented' different ways of getting round the problem. Cameras were positioned at unusual angles -- above interviewees' heads or by their ears -- or shots were cut away to focus on the movements of their hands, which also registered the emotional impact of their words. The technique of 'pixilating' -- blurring a small portion of the screen -- was rejected.

'It's always associated with criminals, or somebody who deserves what they get', explained researcher Simon Cooper.

Other broadcasters have sought different, less controversial approaches to the topic, such as a dramatisation, followed by a studio debate. Belgian director Gil Verhaert proposed the fictional formula for a six-part series on La femme, l'enfant, et la prostitution, in Africa, Asia and Europe. 'We have a lot of information, but we cannot feature the real people because they are all either afraid of the Mafia, or are involved in court cases', he explained. 'Audiences are interested in dramatic events. But it does not have to be sensational. If you keep to the truth, it's more than dramatic enough.'

Many of the journalists reporting on commercial sexual exploitation of children are committed to uncovering what they regard as a profound social evil: 'We have a role to play in increasing awareness', says Aart Zeeman. 'It's such a disgusting thing'.

The work of such media professionals not only acts as a counter-weight to media indifference and lack of awareness, it adds to the resources available to campaigners. The material produced may be linked in with campaigns on the issue by local NGOs, or destined for educational use -- as in the case of Gil Verhaerts project.

He hoped his work might be used in the Philippines among families who sell their own children into prostitution. In Bangkok, a campaign has been launched to show parents the horrors their daughters would face in the sex trade.

5. FREEDOM OF EXPRESSION AND THE CHALLENGE OF SELF-REGULATION

Journalists tend to be wary of regulators. They have much evidence to support the view that intervention in the affairs of journalism inevitably leads to forms of censorship. However, it is a legitimate question whether media self-regulation is a sufficient answer to public concern over standards of journalism in an age when the changing media landscape, and particularly the growth of global media enterprises appears, in theory at least, to put media beyond the range of national public accountability.

Effective self-regulation, by which the errors of media professionals are dealt with by their peers, may not be so convincing when media organisations appear to use professional codes to support their particular interests, which in a commercial system of mass communication by no means necessarily coincide with those of journalism or the public interest. There has been in the past criticism that self-regulation has been used to provide what might be called a 'social alibi' for the mass media industry, that is to prevent society from taking more definite (legal) measures.

This argument goes to the heart of the uncomfortable balance of interests which prevails in today's media -- that ethical standards are being sacrificed in defence of commercial interests. One of the principle problems lies in the implementation and enforcement of rules. Very often even regulatory bodies lack the power to enforce sanctions which bite. In Canada in 1990, the CBC's Equity Task Force found that, with regard to equitable employment and portrayal, self-regulation and incentive measures have failed to accomplish desired and anticipated results.

Some professional codes aspire to the very highest moral standards, as in Chile, journalism and journalists must be in the service of truth, social justice, human rights and the ideals of the improvement of society and of peace among peoples.

And there is no doubt that many individuals, like those quoted above, are committed to exposing and condemning sexual exploitation. Sadly, many more choose to reflect the commercial or political interests of advertisers, proprietors, or political parties.

This control seldom takes the form of direct intervention or censorship, but far more often of self-censorship by the media professionals themselves - who may not even be aware that they are exercising it.

In an Indiana University School of Journalism study in the 1980s, 88% of the journalists questioned said they acquired their ethical values from the newsroom itself. Aidan White identifies several extra factors which encourage "the tendency towards self-censorship and self-denial of social responsibility" among media professionals, including: the growth of new technologies, which threaten to overwhelm existing regulatory structures, or the unaccountable nature of transnational media corporations which evade terrestrial control of media standards, or the increasingly insecure working environment in which journalists work.

Journalists' unions who have tried to enforce their own ethical standards through disciplinary proceedings, have found themselves in the tricky if not impossible position of attacking individual workers they exist to support.

Despite all this, codes and guidelines still have a crucial role to play, in raising awareness and providing a model of good practice. In Spain, in 1993, for example, regional and national broadcasting organisations joined with the national and regional Education Ministries in agreeing Self-regulation Principles for Television Channels concerning the specific content of their programmes with regard to protecting children and young people. The document recognises 'the significant role which television plays in Spanish society and its influence on society, particularly children and young people. Specific guidelines on reporting child abuse could be drawn up by professional associations to accompany their general ethical codes, along the lines of guidelines for reporting AIDS published by the NUJ (UK and Ireland).

In the final analysis, the support of media employers and regulators is crucial to improving newsroom values as highlighted by Cheryl Lai: Much of the biased or sensationalist coverage, especially headlines, is created by editors, and it will be difficult to gain improvements given Taiwan's patriarchal society unless high-level media editors and managers implement such a policy from the top down.

Attitudes to censorship and freedom of expression vary widely from country to country and culture to culture. In all countries, broadcasting tends to be more highly regulated than newspapers and magazines. The importance of the right to freedom of expression cannot be underestimated, yet it is not without boundaries. Both the UN Universal Declaration of Human Rights and the European Convention for the Protection of Human Rights and Fundamental Freedoms draw attention to the responsibilities accompanying this right, including respect for the rights or reputations of others'.

The question of freedom of expression is relevant in particular to child pornography. Can there be a distinction between pornography, and the justifiable portrayal of 'childhood sexuality' in works of art? Amy Adler argues that the US Supreme Court, in its anxiety to protect children, has thrown out 'important speech-protective features of the law', including 'the traditional protection afforded to artistic expression'.

But American lawyer Andrew Vachss, a specialist in child abuse cases, believes that the controversy over art is a red herring thrown up by the paedophile community.

The issue is not 'what is art?' but 'what is victimisation?' I can no more accept a child pornographer saying he is a victim of censorship than I could a mugger claiming his field of activity was performance art.

The issue of rights to freedom of expression cannot be ignored, but should be turned around to focus first on the rights of the child to freedom from fear and exploitation. As June Kane points out, 'Journalists should, as always, look at the facts, and have at their fingertips the medical and other evidence to prove that the commercial sexual exploitation of children cannot be justified.

6. BUILDING IMAGES OF CHILDREN, SEX AND VIOLENCE IN THE MEDIA

There is increasing alarm in a number of countries that the way children are portrayed by the media today may increase the risks they face. Controversy continues internationally about how far children's behaviour is influenced by what they see on television - particularly with regard to violence.

The loudest recent public controversy about the portrayal of children has focused recently on the American film Kids, directed by Larry Clark. Some critics condemned the film as voyeuristic, and expressed disbelief that the young actors, mostly amateur, who enacted the film's brutal sexual encounters, were themselves above the age of consent. The film raised worrying questions both about the exploitation of increasingly youthful actors, and about the impact on young audiences who might regard the characters as role-models. In some countries, the film was barred to under-18s. The crucial question is whether adults themselves are encouraging children to become prematurely sexually active, or to seem to be so.

This question is particularly relevant to pop music and modelling which are two of the most influential industries among young people today. In fashion, it is the woman-child' who now rules the catwalk.

Gianne Albertoni Vicente is 5ft 10in, with long blond hair, wide-apart eyes and wonderful bones. Oh, and she's only 13.

The recent revelation that a 12-year-old schoolgirl had been signed up by an adult modelling agency in the UK, with the approval of her parents, caused widespread soul-searching in the media. Was it a harmless bit of fun, or the symptom of a dangerous trend? The commentators disagreed, but most expressed alarm. Even the girl's mother admitted that there was a 'sexual angle'; expanded upon by psychologist Dorothy Rowe:

There is something intriguing about the young girl who is just discovering life and is beginning to wonder what it's all about. It is the kind of titillation in which a virginal girl intrigues a man. In areas of sexuality intended to intrigue, it is especially dangerous because the child is being presented with issues that they are not really ready to deal with, no matter how precocious they look.

British Member of Parliament Ann Winterton judged it to be a 'trend almost verging on the paedophilic'. The fear must be that, the more grown-up women are persuaded to aspire to having a childlike body, the more the distinction between adults and children, also with respect to sexuality, will become blurred.

Then, in May, the watch-manufacturer Omega announced that it planned to withdraw advertising from a major fashion magazine, Vogue, in protest at the use of waif-like models. Within a couple of weeks, Omega had obtained more publicity - all of it free and much of it highly complimentary - than a year's worth of advertising in magazines. Ironically, the threat was withdrawn on the instructions of the chairman Nicolas Hayek, ostensibly in the interest of press freedom. Omega's brand director Giles Rees wrote to Vogue:

I would hope that the tremendous support and encouragement that we have received from the media and particularly from the public would urge you to consider addressing these issues with your editorial staff.

If it can be demonstrated to companies that they have something to gain in terms of public approval and financial return from rejecting sexually exploitative images, this might have a major impact.

The impact of public pressure on the media, on this issue as any other, should not be underestimated. Parents and educators in France, for instance, have been urged to react when TV stations show material lacking in respect for children, whether or not it is intended for young viewers. In Australia, a national campaign to improve the portrayal of women in the media included the distribution of information packs telling audiences how to complain about what they heard or saw.

Jennifer Rowe, former editor of the Australian Womens Weekly, commented: In the end, all media are driven by their ratings or their readership, and if they can see that they are losing that, by persisting in an attitude that is outmoded, they will change.

The most fascinating aspect of the model controversy is how it was handled by the newspapers themselves. The girl's first appearance, according to Alexander Chancellor, was on the front page of the Daily Telegraph.

The next day she was taken up by the tabloids. She was pouting and smouldering in the photographs in an alarmingly grown-up way. The tabloids were thrilled of course, but also censorious.

Indeed, its professed outrage did not stop the Daily Mail from reprinting a full-length picture of the girl in her 'smouldering' modelling pose, under the heading 'Who on earth would allow a child of 12 to pose like this?' It might have queried, more relevantly, who on earth would publish a picture of her doing it. And as if to reinforce the sexual message, the feature was placed next to a small beauty item giving advice on how to achieve 'a perfect pout'. The morally self-righteous stance adopted by some sections of the media is directly contradicted when it come to stories and images that make money.

For the popular music industry, international TV channels like MTV, where pop videos make up a large proportion of output, are a very significant means of reaching young people and children - even those too young to attend concerts or buy CDs. Professor Monique Remy analysed the images of young people in these videos.She found:...stereotyped masculine and feminine images, sado-masochistic scenes, Asian exoticism, fetishist female garments, women as bloodsuckers and trouble- makers, both men and women grotesquely made-up, with an element of androgyny.

Women appeared as child-like, asexual yet provocative, dangerous, yet also victimised. In their analysis of 166 videos broadcast by MTV, WTBS and NBC in 1984, Barry Sherman and Joseph Dominick drew attention to the provocative style of dress, and the portrayal of young women as either aggressors or victims.

The Council of Europe's experts also warned of the 'insidious' exploitation of children's and young people's bodies in show business and the media, and the use of children's pictures or voices to create an erotic atmosphere.

'Lolitas' (both male and female) seem to have come back into fashion in the cinema and show business, appealing to the unwholesome taste of a certain section of the public.

Certainly some media commentators have perceived this as evidence of a 'widespread phenomenon.. ..of confusion over the boundary between adults and children', in which parents have colluded in the sexual exploitation of their children.

We inhabit a culture which makes a great deal of money out of the mass premature sexualisation of children. Their music, their clothes, the TV and films they watch and the teen magazines they read envelop them in a miasma of sexuality ....Children who are glued to the set have been turned into voyeurs at the peepshow of adult behaviour.... Popular culture presents to them as normal a brutally crude, mechanistic world in which sexual gratification is another commodity, available not just to adults but to them, along with the clothes, CDs and cosmetics.

Little wonder then, the argument goes, that if the media consistently present young and old audiences alike with images of children in a sexual context, some adults will believe that children are ready and able to participate in sexual activity.

Our society panics about an apparent epidemic of child sexual abuse. Does it ever occur to anyone that maybe there is some connection with the multinational business of precocious child sexuality?

Rachel O'Brien believes it is dangerous to view these developments as 'Armageddon' - a catastrophic loss of innocence about which nothing can be done. But she does perceive a widespread confusion about what childhood means, and points out that the definition of childhood itself differs from community to community, and age to age. Children are aware of their bodies, and do need to explore and learn about sex. But this should be done gradually, in a tolerant, safe environment; through natural contact with other children, and with the support of parents.

The problems, she says, arise from adults looking at young people in a certain way: appropriating them for their own use. They create exploitative and, in extreme cases, paedophile images. The image of pre-pubescent children offering themselves for sex allows adults to claim that they are responsible for the provocation. "How do young people themselves consume these images? On the one hand, many children are denied sex education, while on the other there is a glorification of children in provocative poses. It seems that either we want our children to be totally innocent, or to be prostitutes. And the whole question of their rights as individuals gets left out.'

All this makes the notion of a 'youth oriented society' into a slogan of little substance, concludes George Gerbner. The media are oriented towards 'markets and power' rather than youth. Advertisers focus on consumers and potential consumers - and we will look at advertising specifically later in this paper. But in television output children have no power. They 'take on the characteristics of a social minority with less than their share of attention, values, and resources, and consequently diminished life chances.'

The solution may be simple to see, but not so easy to achieve. That is, to give a voice in the media to children themselves, to listen to their views and aspirations.And to educate them to be knowledgeable and critical about how the media work. International conventions and recommendations already emphasise the right of children to have a say in decisions affecting them, and call for a change in the way children are regarded . The Draft Declaration from this Congress also emphasises that children have a right to express their views on matters affecting their lives, and calls for children's participation in action (Article 6). Why should children not also have more say in the media? Dr Ulla Bjrnerg proposes documentary programmes on young peoples lives in different countries, with the aim of giving children aged from 7 to 18 - including poor and migrant children - an opportunity to air their opinions.

Washington Post journalist Tom Wilkinson points out the importance to all newspapers of 'sources'. Children are not regarded as sources because they are not trusted to distinguish accurately between fact and fiction -- a belief that also applied to children giving evidence in court until recently. New means of giving children access to the media as sources should be investigated, perhaps through the mediation of child help lines, with reassurance that information offered would be strictly confidential.

Wilkinson also makes the crucial point that: child abuse does not fall squarely into a specific area of reporting. Is it part of the police beat, medicine, sociology, or government? The Post doesn't have a child abuse reporter per se, and I doubt that any major newspaper does.

We have already seen, in Taiwan, the difference in approach when the topic is reported by journalists with a broader awareness of social issues. Maybe Wilkinson has hit on the answer. Given the size of the constituency and its importance for the future, should not news media have specialist 'children's correspondents', with a brief covering all aspects of children's lives, and specific training to enable journalists to express the child's point of view? Maybe this would do most to 'promote change in the traditional view of the child'. In its report on implementation of the Council of Europe Recommendation No.R (91)11, the British government suggests the sort of training that would be appropriate for 'all professionals who come into contact with children', including: self-awareness, children's sexual terminology, child growth and development, child abuse, risk factors, the law, interviewing techniques, communication with children, and video recording.

The British Home Office also decided to produce a 'good practice' video for judges and lawyers. Governments or NGOs might consider making good practice videos for editors and journalists. Another measure to assist journalists in covering children's issues seriously and accurately would be for NGOs in each country to compile a directory of reliable experts on different topics, which could be available on every news desk.

International bodies have called for more information to be given to children- both through the media and at school - about the dangers and risks of sexual exploitation, and how to defend themselves. But children, from primary school upwards, also need media literacy training, to help them understand and decode the messages they receive from both programmes and advertising, so as to become critical and well-informed media consumers. In Canada, for instance, the organisation Mediawatch

The survey asked whether self-regulatory bodies had received any reaction from viewers to the use of naked children. Only four: Ireland, France, Portugal and the UK, reported any specific response, with viewers in the UK in particular complaining that such images would be regarded by paedophiles as erotic titillation.

Henry Danthan believes advertisers now understand the need to adopt high standards in advertising for and by children. Yet the fact remains that shock adverts, like the Calvin Klein example, attract massive extra publicity.

In the end, there are two other problems with the concept of self-regulation, highlighted by Simon-Pierre De Coster, a legal advisor with the Belgian broadcaster RTBF. The first is that mechanisms are only equipped to deal with grave breaches of regulations. But it is not the grave cases that are the main problem, he points out. It is the accumulative effect of banal stereotypes that are used everyday without sanction.

Secondly, advertising codes rely on notions such as 'good taste', 'bad taste' and 'decency'. But how are these terms to be interpreted and implemented? 'What is the broadcaster to make of these texts? They should be defined somewhere'. Both media workers and the public have a crucial role to play in indicating where the bounds of acceptability are drawn, and consumer boycotts of products can have a powerful effect: The mere threat of such action is already effective insofar as a television station is very reluctant to risk seeing a source of advertising revenue diminish or disappear.

But while efforts continue to try to set standards in the existing world of media technology, the development of new forms of communication such as the Internet has opened up new opportunities for paedophiles and pornographers which have brought international concern. Men exchange pornographic accounts of their exploits as sex tourists, for example, supplying details of bars, brothels, and prices.

In 1995, Thailand's Tourist Authority tried to take action to delete graphic details of sex venues and massage parlours from Netscape: The World

Sex Guide. The Internet contributor was identified as a 50-year-old American, Bruce Cassirer, who had also written a 'travel guide' on where to find young prostitutes. Cassirer was declared persona non grata by Thailand, and a warrant issued for his arrest.

Governments have now discovered that the major problem in controlling material on the Internet, is that nobody controls it. In France, net providers went on strike to obtain an assurance from the Ministry of Telecommunications that they were not to blame for child pornography. The Association of French Internet Professionals demanded a legal debate to establish who was responsible for the material. In the United States free-speech campaigners have won in recent days an injunction against official attempts control content on the Internet.

Whatever media strategies may emerge in the campaign for children's rights, they will have to be linked to this rapidly-changing media environment, and one that offers much less scope for control and regulation than before.

8. CONCLUSIONS AND RECOMMENDATIONS

The International Federation of Journalists, in its proposed amendment to the Draft Declaration of this Congress, called for action to encourage media professionals to develop strategies which strengthen the role of media in providing information of the highest quality, reliability and ethical standards concerning all aspects of the commercial sexual exploitation of children. The following recommendations are designed to strengthen the key role of journalists in revealing instances of abuse, and also in monitoring the performance of national and international bodies, both in honouring their commitments and working to end the commercial sexual exploitation of children.

There are some simple but practical points to bear in mind here. The media can, without doubt, influence the decision-makers. But to do this effectively, media professionals must choose how and when. For broadcasters, for example:

Time is critical... First, the reporter needs enough air time to present the subject properly. Second, the story must be broadcast at a time when the people who ought to see it will see it. Finally, a sense of social timing is essential. Just as some entertainment shows will sell one year and not the next, so too with news stories; audiences are not static in their responsiveness to social issues.

Matters relating to children have traditionally featured more often in women's magazines and programmes. If children's exploitation is to be given the priority it demands, it must be highlighted in all media, particularly those which reach opinion formers and people taking decisions. This is an issue which touches on the economy, society, education, development, and the environment and it is one occasion when editors must, as American journalist John Mack Carter admits, 'strive to present material that not only captures the imagination but also prompts action'.

Recommendations For Further Action

1. Training for journalists

a) Ethical questions should have a higher profile in journalists' training, particularly with regard to standards of conduct in reporting issues like children's exploitation.

2 Codes of Conduct and Self Regulation

a) While codes of conduct and guidelines appear not to be effective, they can be useful in demonstrating that something needs to be done. Such codes are weapons in the hands of journalists and campaigners who can use them to take up issues with editors, publishers and broadcasters.

b) Specific guidelines on reporting child abuse could be drawn up by professional associations to accompany their general ethical codes.

c) In preparing this report, the Confederation of ASEAN Journalists suggested that further study on this issue, by media professionals in the regions. Such further activity is highly recommended.

3. Media organisations and Media Professionals

a) Journalists and programme-makers have a duty to increase public awareness of the dangers of the commercial sexual exploitation of children. However, reporting needs to be carried out with enormous care.

b) Journalists and programme-makers should adhere to the highest standards of professional conduct when confronted with dilemmas such as professional secrecy, the use of subterfuge, and the identification of victims, in the course of their duties.

c) They should avoid, or challenge, the myths and stereotypes which surround children, and particularly children from developing countries. For instance, the myth that parents in developing countries do not value their children; that girls are inferior to boys; that children are drawn into vice through their own fault; or that sex tourism alleviates poverty for the victim, or the host nation.

d) Media professionals should recognise that freedom of expression must go hand in hand with other fundamental human rights, including freedom from exploitation and intimidation. They should give careful consideration to the facts when weighing up the relative merits of the different claims, and not allow themselves to be swayed by commercial or political considerations.

e) Journalists should never publish details which help exploiters to find their victims, or which undermine the safety of child victims. Journalists should take particular care not to reveal information which could lead to the collapse of criminal proceedings against exploiters.

f) Journalists and programme-makers should look for innovative ways to respect the dignity of child victims, and avoid identifying them, while at the same time telling their stories in a compelling and newsworthy way. For instance, by consulting them on the content or showing ways in which they can escape from their situation. They should try to focus attention not only on the victims of commercial sexual exploitation, but on the perpetrators and clients.

4. The Need for Newsroom Debate

a) A constructive and supportive debate should be encouraged between media professionals, about how this issue should be investigated and reported.

b) Media organisations should consider appointing specialist 'children's correspondents', with responsibility for covering all aspects of children's lives. Specific training to help journalists to express children's points of view. This might include: child growth and development, child abuse, risk factors, children's sexual terminology, the law, interviewing techniques, communication with children, etc.

c) New means of giving children access to the media, as 'sources' or commentators, should be investigated. Children should know that information or opinions offered in confidence will be protected as such.

5. The Role of Management

a) Media editors and managers should implement -- from the top down -- a policy which makes clear their opposition to biased and sensationalist coverage of the

commercial sexual exploitation of children, and their support for high ethical standards among journalists and programme-makers. This could be done through the elaboration, in consultation with media professionals, of ethical guidelines on this and other issues, which should be seriously implemented and monitored.

6. Governments and NGOs

a) Governments or NGOs should support efforts by media organisations and journalists' associations to raise awareness. In this regard, good practice videos for editors and journalists would be useful.

b) In particular, support should be given to national women's media associations, such as those existing in many African countries, which are taking up the issue of media coverage of violence and violations of the rights of children.

c) National NGOs should consider compiling a directory of reliable experts on commercial sexual exploitation of children, and related topics, to be distributed to media. Such information could also be accessible on computer data banks.

7. Children and the Community

a) Children, from primary school upwards, should undergo media literacy training, to help them understand and decode the messages they receive from both programmes and advertising, so as to become critical and well-informed media consumers.

b) The public should recognise and use their power, as audiences and consumers, to affect media policy, for instance through lobbying and consumer boycotts. ●

International Federation of Journalists , Brussels, June 15th 1996

Referecnces

Alston, P., 1994, The best interests principle, in Alston, P., (ed.), The Best Interests of the Child: Reconciling culture and human rights, Oxford, Clarendon Press

Agarwal, Bina, 1981, Agricultural Modernisation and Third World Women, ILO, Geneva

Agroforestry Report, Agroforestry Basic Health Collective, n.d. Situational analyses report on girls trafficking in Sindhupalchowk, Mahankal and Inchowk Village Development Committee, Nepal: Agroforestry Basic Health Co-operative.

Asia Partnership for Human Development. 1985. Awake. Sydney: APHD.

.........1992, Awake 2, Philippines: APHD.

Asia Watch, 1993, A Modern Form of Slavery Trafficking of Burmese Women and Girls into Brothels in Thailand, New York: Human Rights Watch.

Bahni, 1989, Prostitution with religious sanction: The devadasi problem, Venkatasani, Jogini and the Basavi cult, New Delhi: Joint Women's Project.

Bannerjee, Sumanta, 1979,Child Lab0ur in India, Anti Slavery Society, Child Labour Series. Report No 2, London

Barse, S., (1991), Rights of the girl child, in: Indian Journal of Social Work, LII, and 1 (97 104).

Bell, L, 1987, Good Girls/Bad Girls: Feminists and Sex Trade Workers Talk Face to Face Toronto: The Women's Press.

Black, M., 1991, Philippines: Children of the Runaway Cities. Florence: UNICEF.

In the Twilight Zone, Child workers in the hotel, tourism and catering industry, 1995, International Labour Office, Geneva

Blanchet, T., 1996, Lost innocence, stolen childhood, Dhaka: The University Press Limited.

Bond, T., 1981, Boy Prostitution in Sri Lanka, Colombo: Terre des Hommes,

Campagna, D. S. & Poffenberger, D.L. 1988 The Sexual Trafficking in

Children. Dover, Massachusetts: Auburn House Publishing Company.

Carman, J.B. & Marglin, F.A., 1985, Purity and auspiciousness in Indian Society, International Studies in Sociology and Social Anthropology (43), Leiden. E. J. Brill.

Chambers, Robert, 1982 "Health, Agriculture and Rural Poverty: Why Seasons matter", in Journal of Development Studies Vol18.no.2 (January)

Constantine L., and Martinson, F.M., (eds.), 1981, Children and Sex: New Findings, New Perspectives, Boston: Little, Brown and Company

Dallape, F., 1988, An experience with street children, Nairobi, Undugu Society.

Dhital. R, 1992,Child Prostitution in Nepal, CWIN, Kathmandu

ECPAT Philippines, 1994, Tourism and Child Prostitution in Cebu, Manila: ECPAT.

ECTWT (Ecumenical Coalition on Third World Tourism), 1983, Tourism, Prostitution, Development, Bangkok: ECTWT.

Ennew, J. 1986. The Sexual Exploitation of Children. Cambridge: Polity.

ESCAP, Promotion of Community Awareness for the Prevention of Prostitution, 1991,New York

Fernand-Laurent, J., 1983, Report of the Special Rapporteur on the Suppression of the Traffic in Persons and the Exploitation of the Prostitution of Others, Geneva: United Nations.

Fernand-Laurent, J., 1992, The mass media and sexual exploitation, in Children Worldwide, 19 (2), p. 36.

Galanter, M., 1989, Law and Society In Modern India, Oxford: Oxford University Press.

Gathia. Joseph, 1994, Market Economy and Children, Centre of concern for Child Labour, New Delhi, unpublished manuscript.

Goonesekere, S., & Abeyratne, 1986, Child labour and child prostitution in Sri Lanka, in Report of the Conference on Child Labour and Prostitutes in the Philippines, Manila: Law Asia.

Ghose.S.K., Women and Crime, 1993, Ashish Publications ,New Delhi

Gulati Leela, 1981, Profiles in Female Poverty, Delhi

Government of India Fourth World conference on Women in Beijing-Country Report 1995,New Delhi

Human Rights Watch, 1995, Rape for Profit, New York: Human Rights Watch.

Jahangir, A., Prostitution of Children in Pakistan, Undated, Lahore

Jubilee Action Trust, n.d., Child Prostitution in Thailand, London: Jubilee Trust.

Kent, G., 1992, Little foreign bodies: International dimensions of child prostitution, in Freeman, M., & Veeran, P., (eds.), The ideologies of children's rights, Netherlands: Kluwer Academic Publishers, (323-346).

Lee-Wright, P. 1990. Child Slaves. London: Earthscan Publications.

Lowman, J. 1987,Taking Young Prostitutes Seriously, In Canadian Review of Sociology And Anthropology, 24, (1) (99-116).

Marglin, F.A., 1985, Wives of the god king: the rituals of Devadasis of Puri, Oxford: Oxford University Press.

Melton, G.B., 1991, preserving the dignity of children around the world, in Child Abuse and Neglect, 15, (343-350).

Meccaughy, C.H., & Hou, C., 1994, Family Affiliation and Prostitution in a Cultural-Context: Career Onsets of Taiwanese Prostitutes, in Archives of Sexual Behaviour, 23, (3) (251-265).

Moorehead, C, 1989, Betrayal: Child Exploitation In Today's World, London: Barrie & Jenkins.

Moprgan-Thomas, Ruth, The Sex Industry for AIDSAction, 1991, Appropriate Health Resourcesand Technologies Action Group

Mowli, V.C., "Jogin": Giri child labour studies, New Delhi: Sterling Publications Private Ltd.

Muecke, M.A., 1992, Mother Sold Food, Daughter Sells Her Body: The Cultural Continuity of Prostitution, in Social Science and Medicine, 35, (7) (891-901).

Muntabhorn, V., 1992, Sale of Children, Report submitted by the United Nations Special Rapporteur on the Sale of Children, New York: United Nations E/CN.4/1992/55.

Narvesen, O., 1989, The Sexual Exploitation of Children in Developing Countries, Oslo: Redd Barna.

National Consultation on Adolescent Prostitution, 1984, Proceedings of the National Consultation on Adolescent Prostitution, Ottawa: Canada

O'Connell Davidson, J., & Brace, L., 1996, Desperate Debtors and Counterfeit Love: The Hobbesian World of the Sex Tourist, Leicester: Leicester University Department of Sociology.

O'Dea, P., 1993, Gender exploitation and violence: the market in women, girls and sex in Nepal, Kathmandu: UNICEF.

O'Grady, R., 1992, The Child and the Tourist, Bangkok: ECPAT.

--------------- 1994, The Rape of the Innocent, Bangkok: ECPAT.

Patkar, P., 1991, The girl child in red light areas, in Indian Journal of Social Work, LII (1) (71-80).

Pelzer, K., n.d., Children as commercial farm labourers and prostitutes in Africa, ANPPCAN Conference on Child Labour.

Phongpaichit, P., 1982, From Peasant Girls to Bangkok Masseuses, Geneva: International Labour Office.

Reich, Robert B. Forced Labour: The Prostitution of Children 1996,US Department of labour, Washington

Richards, M., 1996, When is puberty? Seminar paper, Centre for Family Research, University of Cambridge, May 1996.

Risaluddin, S., 1996, Moral and ethical concerns for the sexual health and safety of children: Islamic scriptural, traditional and cultural perspectives, paper for WCRP/UNICEF, March 1996, New York.

Rozario, A. de, 1989, The Street Girls of Metro Manila, Vulnerable Victims of Today's Silent Wars: A Situation Study on Street Girls, Manila: Childhope Asia.

Rozario, Rita. 1988, Trafficking in Women and Children in India: Sexual Exploitation and Sale Uppal, New Delhi

Sachs, A., 1994, The Last Commodity: Child Prostitution in the Developing World, in World Watch, 7, (4) (24-30).

Salinlahi, Inc, Gabriela, Bahay Tuluyan and Family Ministries Program, n.d., Child Prostitution and Tourism, Philippines: unpublished manuscript.

Sawyer, R., 1988, Children Enslaved, London: Routledge.

Scheper-Hughes, N., and Stein, H., 1987, Child Abuse and the Unconscious in American Popular Culture, in Schepper-

Hughes, N. (ed.), Child Survival: anthropological perspectives on the treatment and maltreatment of children Dordrecht; Lancaster: Reidel

Sereny, G., 1984, The Invisible Children: Child Prostitution in America, West Germany and Great Britain, London: Andre Deutsch.

Sittitrai, W., and Brown, T., 1994, The Impact of HIV on Children in Thailand, Bangkok: Thai Red Cross Society.

Shankar,J., 1994 ,Devadasi Cult ; A Sociological Analysis, Ashish Publishing House, New Delhi

Tate, T., 1991, Child pornography: an investigation, London: Methuen.

Treguear, T. & Carro, C., 1994, Ninas y Adolescents Prostituidas, San Jose, Costa Rica: UNICEF, Childhope, PRONICE.

Truong, T.D., 1982, The Dynamics of Sex Tourism, in Development and Change 14, (4) (533-553).

Vittachi, A.., 1989,Stolen Childhood, Cambridge: Polity Press

Weisberg, D. K., 1985, Children of the Night: A Study of Adolescent Prostitution. Massachusetts: Lexington Books.

INDEX